Rigby On Our Way to English

Grade 2

Phonics
Teacher's Guide

Language, Literacy, and Content for English Language Learners

Rigby

Language Advisors

Spanish
Elizabeth de la Ossa, Ph.D.
Spanish Educational Publishing, Ltd.

Aurora Colón García
Northside Independent School District (San Antonio), Literacy Specialist

Cecilia Silva, Ph.D.
Texas Christian University

Vietnamese
Phap Dam, Ph.D.
Texas Woman's University

Hmong
Doua Hollie Vu
Fresno Unified School District, Title III Office

Haitian Creole
Flore Zéphir, Ph.D.
University of Missouri–Columbia

Nancy Graham
Miami-Dade County Public Schools, Bilingual Educational Specialist

Cantonese
Beverly Hong-Fincher
University of Kentucky

Helen Yu
New York City Public Schools, Elementary Teacher

Korean
Soohee Kim, Ph.D.
University of Washington

Khmer
Wayne E. Wright
Arizona State University

Russian
Julia Stakhnevich, Ph.D.
Bridgewater State College

Arabic
Younasse Tarbouni
St. Louis University

Tagalog
Maria Sheila Zamar
University of Hawaii at Manoa

On Our Way to English: Phonics Teacher's Guide

Grade 2

© 2004 by Rigby

1000 Hart Road
Barrington, IL 60010
www.rigby.com

Editor-in-Chief: Judy Nyberg; Executive Editors: Lynelle H. Morgenthaler and Sandy Petroshius; Curriculum Advisor: Clara Amador-Watson; Conceptual Design: Lynelle H. Morgenthaler; Design Director: Jeff Wills; Marketing Product Manager: Marilyn Lindgren; Supervising Editors: Eduardo Aparicio, Anne Kaske, Robert McCreight, Nina Tsang, Arianne Weber; Senior Editors: Karen Clevidence, Cathy Tell, Elizabeth Yoder; Editors: Judi Black, Sophia Caribacas, Lisa Chesters, Meg Garcia, Megan Healy, Jennette McClain, Sue Schumer, Mary Susnis, Loretta West; Design Manager: Jackie Ropski; Supervising Designers: Ann Cain, Julie Spielman, Judy Tresnowski; Senior Designer: Phil Meilinger; Designers: Noel Arreola, Michael Beckett; Image Manager: Cecily Rosenwald; Art and Photo Coordinator: Karen McKinlay; Production Manager: Tom Sjoersma; Production Specialist: Gwen Plogman; Graphic Services Administrator: Stuart Cook; Publishing Operations Manager: Alayne Zahara; Senior Project Coordinator: Rachel Bachman; Business Associate: Karen Savord; Manufacturing Manager: Theresa Wiener; Manufacturing Coordinators: Tom Behrendt, Vanessa Kirk

All rights reserved. No part of this publication may be reproduced or transmitted in any form or by any means, electronic or mechanical, including photocopying, recording, taping, or any information storage and retrieval system, without permission in writing from the publisher.

09 08 07 06 05 04 03
10 9 8 7 6 5 4 3 2 1

Printed in China

ISBN 0-7578-7883-0

Program Authors

David Freeman   Yvonne Freeman

Dr. Yvonne S. Freeman and Dr. David E. Freeman are professors in the Department of Curriculum and Instruction in the School of Education at University of Texas–Pan American. Yvonne is a professor of bilingual education, and David is a professor of reading. They are interested in literacy education for English language learners. In addition to doing staff development with school districts across the country, they present regularly at international, national, and state conferences. They have published articles on the topics of second language teaching, biliteracy, bilingual education, and second language acquisition. They have coauthored several books together, including *Closing the Achievement Gap, Teaching Reading in Multilingual Classrooms, Between Worlds, Teaching Reading and Writing in Spanish in the Bilingual Classroom,* and *ESL/EFL Teaching Principles for Success.*

Lydia Stack

Lydia Stack is an administrator at the Bilingual Education and Language Academy of the San Francisco Unified School District. She also teaches courses at San Francisco State University and Stanford University. She has been an elementary bilingual/ESL teacher and a high school ESL Department Head. She received the San Francisco Star Teacher Award in 1989, California Mentor Teacher twice, and the CATESOL Sadie Iwataki Award for outstanding service to the profession. She was the 1991–1992 President of TESOL (Teachers of English to Speakers of Other Languages). She is currently involved in curriculum writing and teacher training and has co-authored three previous educational series: *Voices in Literature, Making Connections,* and *WordWays.*

Aurora Colón García

Aurora Colón García is the literacy specialist for the Northside Independent School District in San Antonio, Texas. She is currently a State Trainer for the Texas First and Second Grade Reading Academies. She has been an instructor at Texas Woman's University, Southwest Texas State University, and the University of Texas at San Antonio. She has been a bilingual teacher, a reading specialist, and an adult ESL instructor. She specializes in early literacy intervention training and is a national literacy consultant. Most recently, she has served as a Program Advisor for Rigby *Colección PM* and has authored several children's books in Spanish and in English.

Mary Lou McCloskey

Mary Lou McCloskey is an international educational consultant and an adjunct professor at Georgia State University. She is the 2002–2003 President of TESOL (Teachers of English to Speakers of Other Languages) and was the 1989–1990 President of Georgia TESOL. She has been an elementary school teacher, an adult reading instructor, and a middle school teacher. She has been awarded the 1999 Moss Chair of Excellence in English at the University of Memphis, TESOL's D. Scott Enright Service Award, and the Georgia TESOL Professional Service Award. Her publications include *Teaching Language, Literature, and Culture, Integrating English, Voices in Literature,* and *Making Connections.*

Cecilia Silva

Cecilia Silva is an associate professor in the School of Education at Texas Christian University in Fort Worth, Texas, and is a member of the Center of Urban Education. Having taught in bilingual/ESL elementary classrooms, she currently specializes in ESL, bilingual, and multicultural education. She is interested in the integration of content area learning and literacy development and is a coauthor of the book *Curricular Conversations: Themes in Multilingual and Monolingual Classrooms.*

Margo Gottlieb

Margo Gottlieb is Director of Assessment and Evaluation for the Illinois Resource Center in Des Plaines, Illinois. Margo has had classroom experience as an elementary ESL and bilingual teacher, has been an administrator of bilingual services, and has served as a consultant for universities, school districts, publishers, and educational organizations. In addition to her involvement in assessment efforts in Illinois, Margo has provided technical assistance to states such as Alaska, Texas, and Pennsylvania. She has also designed state assessments for English language learners in Wisconsin and Delaware.

Contents

What Do English Language Learners Need to Succeed? T6

On Our Way to English Program Structure T7

What Is the Role of Phonics in Teaching English Language Learners? T8

Phonics Lesson Plans T11

Using *On Our Way to English* in Different Classroom Settings T13

Professional Handbook

Developing Children's Oral Language T16

From the Authors

How Do We Teach Phonological Awareness and Phonics to English Language Learners? .T23
Aurora Colón García

Phonics

Scopes and Sequences for Five Languages ...P2

Phonics Skills 1 Through 33 .... P6

Appendix

Appendix A1

What Do English Language Learners Need to Succeed?

As the population of English language learners rises steadily in our schools, teachers and administrators are faced with a complex challenge.

Earlier ideas of language instruction embraced the notion that children needed to speak a language before learning to read it. Now research has shown that literacy and oral language instruction should be integrated from the earliest language learning experiences.

Research has also identified the fact that it takes English language learners an average of five to seven years to catch up to their native-speaking peers in the content areas.

What can we do to help English language learners close the gap between themselves and their native-speaking peers?

How can we teach these children to speak English *while* they are learning to read and *while* they are acquiring content area knowledge?

On Our Way to English was designed specifically to meet these challenges by providing children simultaneous access to English oral language development, comprehensive literacy instruction, and standards-based content area information.

As the triangle to the right shows, content area learning is supported by oral language development and literacy learning. In *On Our Way to English*, whole-class instruction in content area themes bridges from chants, songs, and language-learning games to shared reading texts to hands-on content area activities. Meanwhile children are learning to read through engaging phonics songs and through small-group guided reading experiences that feature texts specifically written for English language learners and that highlight content area topics.

On Our Way to English Program Structure

On Our Way to English Thematic Units, Guided Reading Collection, and Phonics work together to provide the language, literacy, and content instruction necessary to launch English language learners into academic success. The lesson plans in this Teacher's Guide support you in using best practices in language teaching and in literacy instruction. In a step-by-step fashion, the lessons show you how to provide the comprehensible input—instruction that is meaningful to language learners—that these children need in order to succeed. Because the instruction is carefully scaffolded so that each learning experience supports the next, the learning environment in your classroom will become an engaging, motivating arena in which English language learners feel empowered to contribute and achieve.

On Our Way to English—3 key strands

Thematic Units
Guided Reading
Assessment & Evaluation
Phonics

Pacing Chart

Component	Daily Pacing	Block
Thematic Units	30-40 minutes	ESL or ELD block
Phonics	20 minutes	ESL or ELD block
Guided Reading	20 minutes per group	Reading block

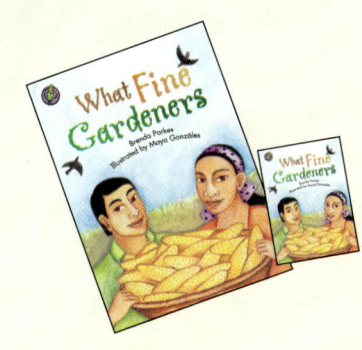

Program Structure On Our Way to English

What Is the Role of Phonics in Teaching English Language Learners?

Phonics is an essential part of any literacy program. *On Our Way to English* Phonics differs from the typical phonics program because it was designed specifically with English language learners in mind. Two elements typically prevent English language learners from being successful with mainstream phonics programs.

First educators are often confused about when phonics instruction is appropriate for English language learners. Phonics is no less important for English language learners than it is for native speakers. At the same time, phonics instruction is meaningless for language learners unless they understand the meaning of the words they are trying to decode. Different elements of phonological awareness and phonics instruction are appropriate at different times during the language learning process. By skillfully guiding the teacher in identifying the level of mastery to be expected of children at each Stage of Language Acquisition, *On Our Way to English* provides the right phonics instruction at the right time.

Because of the general pattern of language acquisition typically (but not always) observed in English language learners, the program's central phonics instruction assumes a gentler pace than the typical mainstream phonics program by focusing on phonological awareness and letter recognition in Kindergarten; consonants and vowels in grade 1; word families, blends, and digraphs in grade 2; and advanced vowel and consonant patterns in grade 3. An Enhanced Phonics offering for grades 1, 2, and 3 provides on-grade-level phonics instruction.

Second mainstream phonics instruction often provides many skill words simultaneously, words that have little context in common. Because language learners remember vocabulary items in linked ways—for instance, the word *bee* might provoke the memory of the words *busy* and *buzz* but not *bat*—the Phonics Song Charts focus on providing fewer skill words that are related through a natural context. Through the medium of song, children are most apt to enjoy and remember the phonics skills they learn.

Phonics Components

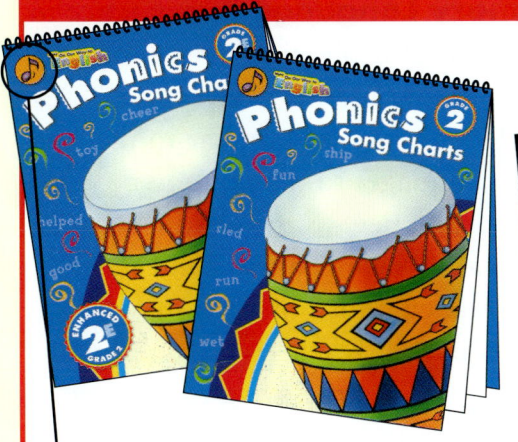

33 Phonics Song Charts
17 Enhanced Phonics Song Charts

33 Take-Home Phonics Stories
17 Enhanced Take-Home Phonics Stories

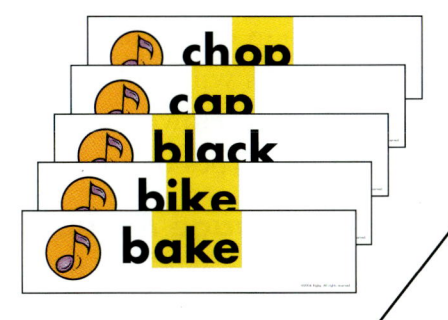

124 Word Wall Cards

Phonics Audio CD
Enhanced Phonics Audio CD

Word Wall Starters integrate the systematic and explicit phonics instruction with thematic unit instruction. Skill labels and word cards are designed to help you jump-start your classroom phonics Word Wall. Cards are provided for skill words in the Phonics Song Chart and for skill words found in the Big Books (available as separate purchase). The words highlighted in the Big Books directly reflect the skills being taught simultaneously in the phonics scope and sequence. Labels help you to organize word families (phonograms) into vowel groupings, such as *short a* and *long a*, and to highlight consonant blends and digraphs.

Phonics Audio CD and **Enhanced Phonics Audio CD** support teachers in introducing and revisiting these songs set to familiar children's tunes.

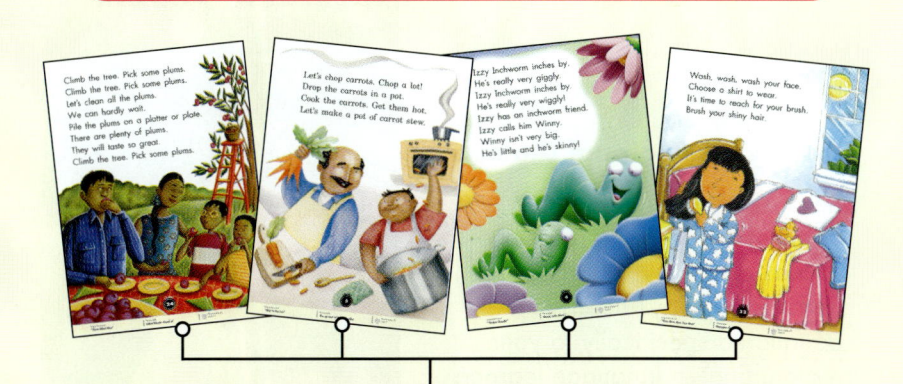

Word Family, **Vowel Review**, **Blend**, and **Digraph Song Charts** help children learn their phonics skills as they sing along to familiar tunes.

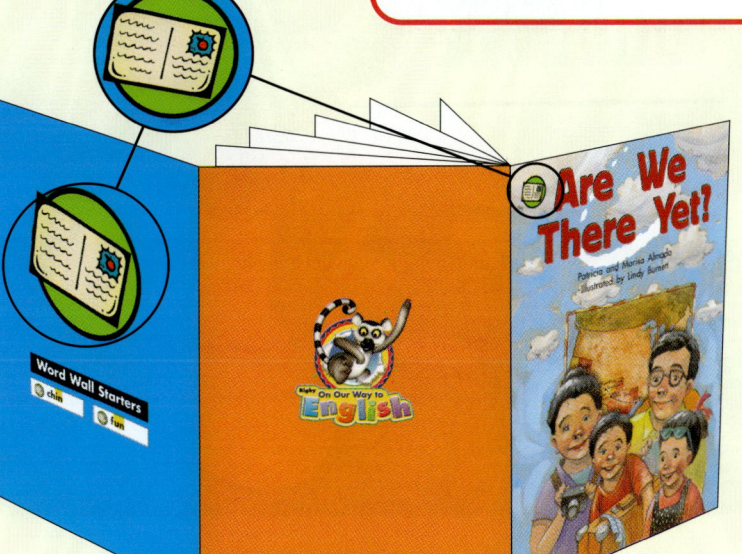

Take-Home Phonics Stories provide text practice for each phonics skill so that children can put the phonics skills they have been learning to work. By encountering the books first at school in small groups, children can feel successful reading the books with family members.

Phonics   On Our Way to English   **T9**

Groupings for Phonics Instruction

The Phonics lesson plans in this Teacher's Guide are designed to support whole-class instruction of English language learners in a mixed group of native languages and English abilities. Most teachers will probably choose to teach phonics in this way. However, the lessons can be modified to suit other types of groupings.

- **Grouping by Stage of Language Acquisition** Some teachers may prefer to group children in similar Stages together and provide phonics instruction at different paces within their classrooms. One option is to work on the grade 2 Phonics Song Charts with children in Stages 1 through 3 and grade 2 Enhanced Phonics Song Charts with children in Stages 4 and 5.

- **Grouping by Primary Language** Best practice in language teaching tells us that phonics instruction for English language learners should move from the known (sounds and letters that are familiar to the child from the native language) to the unknown (sounds and letters that are new to the child). For many teachers, the wealth of languages in the classroom makes this impractical. For others, it may be a possibility. Pages P2–5 in this Teacher's Guide provide information on appropriate restructuring of the *On Our Way to English* scope and sequence for use with different language groups. For instance, you can group the Spanish speakers in your classroom together and use the lessons in the order recommended on page P3 under "Spanish."

A Note on Regional Dialects

Because children in different areas of the country pronounce sounds differently, phonics instruction always needs to be tailored specifically to your region. English language learners should learn phonics according to the sounds they hear in everyday speech and are learning to produce.

Phonics Lesson Plans

Creating Comprehensible Input helps you make the chant comprehensible to English language learners line by line.

Singing and Gestures teach children to sing with and gesture to the chant. These techniques help children remember the songs better and, as a result, the phonics skills.

Language Junction supports you in understanding important aspects of your children's primary languages that influence their acquisition of English phonics.

Writing Words puts encoding skills to work through interactive writing that asks children to sound out and write words.

Assessment for Stages provides an appropriate performance assessment for children in each Stage. Finally, you get useful information about the level of mastery to be expected from children in various Stages of Language Acquisition for phonics skills!

Phonics — On Our Way to English — T11

Page P22: The *un* and *ug* Word Families

Chart 9 — Sung to the tune of "Old MacDonald Had a Farm"

> I have fun with my dog, Pug.
> Pug and I play tug.
> Pug and I run in the sun.
> I give Pug a hug.

Setting the Scene
- Bring in a library book about dogs. Tell children that there are many different breeds, or kinds, of dogs, such as collies, cocker spaniels, and sheep dogs. Show them pictures of these dogs. Tell children that a *pug* is another breed of dog. Show the class a picture of a pug and have children tell you one thing they notice about it.

Creating Comprehensible Input
- As you say the chant slowly, use gestures and pointing to make it comprehensible.

I have fun with my dog, Pug.	point to yourself, then point to the dog, Pug
Pug and I play tug.	point to Pug and then to yourself, then make a tugging motion
Pug and I run in the sun.	point to Pug and then to yourself, then run in place
I give Pug a hug.	point to yourself and to Pug, then make a hugging motion

Extending to the *up* and *um* Word Family
Sung to the tune of "Old MacDonald Had a Farm"
> My pup Buttercup eats a plum.
> He barks, "Yum, yum, yum!"
> My pup Buttercup eats it up.
> What a hungry pup!

Singing and Gestures
- Play the song on the Phonics Audio CD and sing along with it together. After children have learned the song, teach them gestures they can make as they sing the song.
- As children sing the first line, have them pretend to pet their dogs.
- On the second line, have children make tugging motions.
- Invite them to run in place as they sing the third line.
- Have children pretend they are hugging their dogs on the last line.

Recognizing the *un* and *ug* Word Families
- Sing the first line of the song, then point to the word *fun* as you say it. Write it on the board or easel pad and say the word again. Point to the letters *un* and tell children that the letters *un* stand for the last two sounds they hear in *fun*. Ask if they can find any other words that sound like *fun*. [*run, sun*] Write the words *run* and *sun* under the word *fun*. Tell children that there are other words that end in /un/. Ask volunteers for any other easy words they can think of that rhyme with *fun*. Bear in mind that only children in Stages 3–5 will be able to brainstorm English words based on sounds.
- Invite children to run in place each time they hear /un/ as you say the following words: *bun, sit, spun, hop, jump, nun, pun, man, pan, run*.
- Continue the routine for words that rhyme with *Pug*.

Exploring Sound-Symbol Relationships
- Use a small sticky note to cover up the first letter of each word on the chart page that ends with *un* or *ug*. This will encourage children to focus on the print of *un* and *ug*.
- After removing the sticky notes, invite children to come up to the chart page and practice underlining the letters that make /un/ and /ug/ with their fingers.

Language Junction
Word-final nasal sounds, /n/, /m/, and /ng/, are much shorter in Cantonese than in English. As a result, native English speakers may have difficulty recognizing the nasal sound a Cantonese-speaking learner of English is trying to produce at the end of a word. Cantonese speakers can be taught to lengthen word-final nasal sounds. Over time, these children will naturally show an improvement in their pronunciation of these sounds.

STAGES: ❶ Preproduction ❷ Early Production ❸ Speech Emergence ❹ Intermediate Fluency ❺ Advanced Fluency

---

Page P23

Writing Words from the *un* and *ug* Word Families
- Encourage children to use their phonics skills in writing. Put away the chart page and write the following sentence on the board or easel pad:
  I have _____ with my dog, _____.
- Ask volunteers to tell you what goes in the first blank. Invite the group to say the word *fun* together, stretching the sounds. Count the number of sounds together as you prepare to write them together.
- Ask children to tell you what letter starts *fun* as you write it down on the board or easel pad. Invite volunteers to come up and write the remaining letters using their phonics skills to match sounds and letters.
- Have children use their own paper to practice writing the letters in the word *fun*.
- Use a similar procedure for the word *Pug* in the second blank in the sentence.
- When you are finished, display the chart page and invite children to make comparisons between the words *fun* and *Pug* on the chart page and the same words on their own papers. Going back to the original print encourages children to use print resources in their spelling.

Using Word Wall Starters
- **Song Chart Words** Display the words *run*, *tug*, and *hug* from the Word Wall Starters pack. Ask if anyone recognizes the words. Compare the words to *run*, *tug*, and *hug* on the chart page. Invite children to tell you what letters are highlighted in yellow on each card. Use the *short u* label to start the short u section of your Word Wall and place the cards *run*, *tug*, and *hug* beneath it, taking care to group word families together. Later as children encounter additional short u words in their reading and other class work, write each new word on an index card and highlight the short u phonogram. Add these words to this section of your Word Wall as well.
- **Big Book Word** Read the Big Book *Are We There Yet?* Then display the word *fun* from the Word Wall Starters pack. Using the word card and the Big Book, use a procedure similar to the one above, and place the word card *fun* beneath the other *un* word family words.

Take-Home Phonics Story
Reading the Book in Class
- Distribute copies of pages 27–28 from the Take-Home Phonics Stories. Have children create their own books.
- For Emergent readers, read one of the books created by a child to a small group of four to six children one or more times. For Early readers, you can skip this step.
- Invite children to buddy read the book in pairs of heterogeneous stages.
- As they seem ready, have children read the book independently.

Word Bank

un		ug	
bun	run	bug	tug
fun	sun	dug	chug
nun	spun	hug	drug
pun	stun	jug	slug
		mug	shrug
		pug	slug
		rug	snug

Assessment for STAGES
- **❶❷** Although these children may participate in word family instruction, they should not be expected to master or apply it.
- **❸** Say the word *fun* and have the child point to the word on the chart page. Identify the letters *un* together and underline them with your finger. Invite him or her to identify which of the following words also belongs to the *un* word family: *cake, bun, cookie*. As desired, use a similar routine for the *ug* word family.
- **❹❺** Say the word *fun* and have the child point to the word on the chart page. Ask him or her to identify the letters *un* and underline them with a finger. Have the child think of another word that has /un/ in it. If he or she needs help, sing the song together and encourage the child to identify a word in the song. As desired, use a similar routine for the *ug* word family.

Connecting to Home
- Tell children to take the books they made home to share with their families once they are able to read them independently.
- Remember to include the Parent Letter from pages 3–10 of the Take-Home Phonics Stories in the appropriate home language when you send home the book made by each child.

Phonics Song Chart 9 — The *un* and *ug* Word Families

Callouts

Word Family lessons provide explicit instruction in using word families (phonograms) to decode words.

Extended Verse allows you to extend the lesson to include additional word families with a similar vowel pattern.

Assessment
- Letter Recognition and Letter Formation, now known to be critical indicators of literacy success, can be assessed on practical forms provided on pages A5–6.

Writing Words moves children from decoding to encoding as you demonstrate how to use phonics skills in writing.

Word Wall Starters make phonics instruction an integral part of your classroom. Children can use your phonics Word Wall as a ready reference that helps them internalize these skills and serves as a spelling resource.

Take-Home Phonics Stories puts children's phonics skills to work in reproducible readers encountered first in the classroom and then brought home to share with families.

Word Bank provides a handy list of words that contain the target phonics skills.

Using *On Our Way to English* in Different Classroom Settings

The Bilingual and Dual-Language Classrooms

In bilingual and dual-language classrooms, children receive some of their daily instruction in their primary language and some in English. Throughout the country, an increasing emphasis on an organized approach to English language instruction is leading bilingual teachers to establish a clear ESL/ELD curriculum. At the same time, interest in dual-language classrooms—in which native English speakers and, for example, native Spanish speakers are brought together in a single classroom to achieve fluency in two languages—is increasing. Children in both these classrooms are usually at several different Stages of English Language Acquisition. Bilingual and dual-language teachers can use *On Our Way to English* in the following ways.

- Begin English-learning instruction with the thematic Units of *On Our Way to English*, tailoring instruction according to the Stages of Language Acquisition present in your classroom.

- Since current research now emphasizes learning to read in both languages simultaneously, you can use the titles in the Guided Reading Collection simultaneous to native-language literacy instruction with all children. The appropriate Literacy Level for a child might be limited by his or her English-speaking ability—do not expect children to be reading at the same Literacy Level in their first and second languages.

- Phonics instruction in English will depend on the Literacy Level of each child in his or her primary language and on the similarity of the writing system of that primary language to English. Children in bilingual programs usually receive phonics instruction in their first language. Use *On Our Way to English* Phonics by focusing first on phonics elements similar to the native language, then moving on to phonics elements that are new, and concluding with phonics elements that pose transfer difficulties. For more information about these elements, refer to the alternate scopes and sequences by language found on pages P2–P5 in the Phonics Teacher's Guide. There is also helpful information about how children's various native languages influence their acquisition of English in the "Language Junction" notes within the lesson plans.

Using *On Our Way to English* in Different Classroom Settings

The Mainstream Classroom

Mainstream classrooms include English language learners at various Stages of Language Acquisition as well as native English speakers. Mainstream classroom teachers can use *On Our Way to English* in the following ways.

- Organize all classroom instruction around the thematic Units in *On Our Way to English*, creating a sense of community and equity for all learners. Use the wide variety of whole-group, small-group, partner, and individual activities provided in the program. This content-based literacy instruction is good instruction for all learners. Tailor activities to the Stages of Language Acquisition present in your classroom.

- Alternatively, you can meet with English language learners for ESL or ELD instruction using the thematic Units while other children participate in independent, collaborative, or center-based activities.

- In your ESL/ELD time, provide *On Our Way to English* Phonics instruction to the whole group of English language learners. However, base your performance expectations on children's Stages of Language Acquisition, as outlined in "Assessment for Stages" within the lesson plans. (See page T10 for other grouping options for Phonics.)

- Meet with small groups of English language learners organized into Rigby ELL Levels for Guided Reading, just as you meet with native speakers for guided reading instruction. All *On Our Way to English* titles can be used with native speakers for mixed-grouping purposes.

The ESL Specialist

In schools with lower populations of English language learners, an ESL specialist may work with children either within the classroom or on a pull-out basis. Communication about instructional objectives and ongoing progress of children with the classroom teacher is essential for achieving academic success for English language learners. Sometimes ESL specialists may choose to combine children from several mainstream classrooms who are at similar Stages of Language Acquisition. Others may choose to group children from one mainstream classroom who are at different Stages. ESL specialists using these different instructional groupings will use the components of *On Our Way to English* differently. ESL specialists can use *On Our Way to English* in the following ways.

- *On Our Way to English* Phonics can be tailored to suit each group's appropriate Stages of Language Acquisition by following the "Options for Stages" and "Assessment for Stages" features within the lesson plans. Teachers working with one or two Stages at a time will hone instruction to only those activities most appropriate for these Stages.

- Work collaboratively with the classroom teacher to ensure that the specially designed Guided Reading Collection titles are used during small-group time within the mainstream classroom within the Reading/Language Arts block.

The Self-Contained Classroom

Self-contained classrooms are made up entirely of English language learners who are at similar Stages of English Language Acquisition, usually Stages 1–3. This homogeneity allows you to create an enriched environment appropriate for the acquisition of language, literacy, and academic content. Keep in mind that, although students may be at the same Stage of Language Acquisition, their Levels of Literacy Development may vary greatly. The self-contained classroom teacher can use *On Our Way to English* in the following ways.

- Use thematic Units for whole-group instruction, following the suggestions in "Options for Stages" within the lesson plans that apply to the Stages of Language Acquisition present in your classroom.

- Group by Rigby ELL Levels for guided reading using the Guided Reading Collection titles designed for English language learners.

- Provide Phonics instruction based on performance expectations for children's Stages of Language Acquisition as outlined in "Assessment for Stages" within the lesson plans. (See page T10 for other grouping options for Phonics.)

Using *On Our Way to English* in Different Classroom Settings

Developing Children's Oral Language

We need to provide instruction that addresses all of the learners' needs simultaneously.

What Does It Mean to Know a Language?

Learning a new language is a complex undertaking. Children must learn English grammar, sounds, word forms, and word meanings (syntax, phonology, morphology, and semantics). They must be able to use the language to communicate in social situations and also to perform demanding academic functions in all content areas as well. They need to understand the kind of language appropriate to a variety of settings and the conventions which regulate communicating effectively within these settings. For academic success, children must be proficient in all four language processes—reading, writing, speaking, and listening *(Peregoy and Boyle 2001; Freeman and Freeman 2001).*

It is important to distinguish between two fundamentally different types of language proficiency. Conversational language, sometimes referred to as Basic Interpersonal Communication Skills (BICS), is social language—often called playground language. It is the language used in making friends, meeting basic needs, and comprehending everyday conversation. BICS is developed relatively rapidly and naturally, much as a child acquires his or her first language, through interaction with native speakers and input that is understandable to the child because of physical and visual context. So conversational language is well supported by context and is not cognitively demanding. BICS takes about two years to develop *(Cummins 2000).*

Academic language, or Cognitive Academic Language Proficiency (CALP), is the type of language necessary for success in school; it is the language of books, math, science, and social studies. It is more complex and abstract, with fewer concrete or visual clues to support meaning. So academic language typically is not well supported by context and is cognitively demanding. CALP is associated with higher-order thinking skills and is only achieved over time through meaningful language, literacy, and content instruction at children's appropriate Stages of Language Acquisition *(Cummins 2000)*. Academic language proficiency takes between five and seven years to develop.

English language learners do not need to develop CALP before content area learning is introduced. Rather, it is integrated language and content instruction that facilitates the simultaneous acquisition of academic language and academic content *(Samway and McKeon 1999)*. English language learners cannot afford to delay important learning in literacy, math, social studies, and science while they wait to acquire BICS first. We need to provide instruction that addresses all of language learners' needs simultaneously so that they can close the achievement gap between themselves and their native-speaking peers.

How Is Language Acquired?

Research has shown that language learners go through a series of predictable stages as they acquire English.

Preproduction These students are fairly new to English and are not yet comfortable producing English speech. The teacher's goal, therefore, is to build English listening comprehension and vocabulary. Children can indicate understanding through gestures, pointing, and nodding and can answer simple *yes/no* questions. Teaching strategies appropriate for this Stage include slowing down and simplifying speech, enunciating clearly, using gestures and body language, repeating and paraphrasing often, avoiding words with multiple meanings, supporting speech with visuals and manipulatives, using captions to label pictures, and Total Physical Response (see page T19). Group activities are especially successful at this Stage. Literacy instruction should focus on reading aloud, shared reading, and shared-to-guided reading.

Early Production These students are just beginning to understand spoken English and are feeling confident enough to produce one- or two-word answers. They can produce set phrases such as greetings. At this Stage, you will want to continue building their receptive vocabulary and motivating them to produce the vocabulary they understand. Techniques appropriate for this Stage are similar to those above. Literacy instruction should focus on reading aloud, shared reading, and shared-to-guided reading.

Speech Emergent These students produce phrases and short sentences. They understand much of the spoken English in the world around them. Despite the errors in their speech, they are able to communicate socially. Academic language is still limited. Strategies appropriate for this Stage include clarifying the usage of words with multiple meanings, using graphic organizers, and supporting speech with visual aids. Encourage children to retell and respond to reading, supporting their efforts with visuals and props. Literacy instruction should focus on reading aloud, shared reading, and guided reading.

Intermediate Fluency These students understand most of the spoken English they encounter. Although their speech is not perfect, communication rarely breaks down. However, they are still struggling to master

Research has shown that language learners go through a series of predictable stages as they acquire English.

Developing Children's Oral Language

> *Children need ongoing opportunities to learn to express ideas in new ways.*

academic language and to expand their abilities in the various content areas. Effective instruction includes the use of strategies such as supporting academic language with graphic organizers or other visual aids. At this Stage, children should be able to understand and communicate with less reliance on manipulatives and real-world objects. Provide opportunities for students to read aloud to others and engage students in meaningful discussions about reading. Literacy instruction should focus on reading aloud, shared reading, and guided reading.

Advanced Fluency These students speak and comprehend spoken English with native-like fluency, although they may still make a few errors with prepositions and idioms. In most educational settings, children at this Stage are transitioned into the mainstream program. However, they may still lag behind their native-speaking peers in academic language and content area knowledge. At this Stage, continue building academic vocabulary and developing higher-order thinking skills and language use in the content areas. Strategies that work well include visual support for academic concepts, opportunities for students to read aloud to others, engaging students in meaningful discussions about reading, and encouraging them to make connections between characters, settings, and ideas across texts. Literacy instruction should focus on reading aloud, shared reading, and guided reading.

While English language learners need to have input that they can understand, they also need to be exposed to language more advanced than they are able to produce in order for their development to progress. Children need ongoing opportunities to learn to express ideas in new ways. Teachers must make efforts to model new language use in increasingly complex contexts.

Meeting the Needs of English Language Learners

English language learners need to be able to use English to communicate in social settings and to achieve academically in all content areas. In order for this to happen, teachers must provide comprehensible input—language that is understandable to language learners because it is contextualized and meaningful—in both oral and written English. Instruction in the language-learning classroom should be contextualized and supported by strategies such as gesturing, restating, and acting out—strategies that enhance and support meaning. In this way, instruction becomes meaningful (in other words, the input becomes comprehensible) to children whose command of English is limited.

Teachers can make instruction comprehensible to students by using the following techniques:

- Using visuals, real-world objects, models, and audiovisual aids as examples of concepts and vocabulary

- Employing gestures, movements, and other body language to emphasize meaning

- Paraphrasing, or saying the same thing in different ways

- Writing key words and ideas on the board or easel pad so that language input is slowed down and children can remember it

> *Our first job as teachers of English language learners is to provide comprehensible input.*

- Using graphic organizers, semantic webs, and charts to show the relationships between ideas

- Checking frequently for understanding and encouraging children to show they understand with gestures, movements, or short answers

- Asking students to explain concepts and vocabulary to one another in small groups or pairs

- Using frequent repetition and restatement

- Keeping oral explanations short and simple

- Connecting to children's prior knowledge and educational experiences

- Using Total Physical Response, a technique in which children respond physically to commands given orally by the teacher or another student

- Using Language Experience Approach (LEA), a technique in which children dictate words, phrases, or sentences about a shared experience to the teacher

- Previewing and reviewing lessons in students' primary language, whenever possible

- Using children as linguistic and cultural resources

(Freeman and Freeman 1998).

Our first job as teachers of English language learners is to provide comprehensible input. Children often go through a silent period (Preproduction). Once they do start to talk, however, we need to respond to their message rather than correct what they say. At the same time, we can model correct language as we interact with English learners. If we constantly correct students, they may become afraid to use their developing English. When asked *Go bathroom?*, the teacher can model the correct language in his or her response without interrupting the purpose of the conversation: *You need to go to the bathroom? Sure, you may do that.*

Similarly, the classroom atmosphere should be one that is inviting and comfortable for language learners. If children are nervous or bored, it is as if a filter goes up and blocks them from learning language. On the other hand, if children are motivated and interested, the filter goes down, allowing language acquisition to take place. This is known as lowering the affective filter. We as teachers need to create a low-anxiety environment in which students feel comfortable taking language-learning risks. Rather than calling on children individually and using traditional tests that may raise the affective filter, we need to engage them in collaborative activities, encourage volunteering, validate attempts to produce language, and use a variety of ways to assess performance.

Children need a comfortable, supportive environment for learning in which they feel confident in taking risks with the new language, are given adequate time for developing higher-order thinking skills and academic language, and receive instruction that fulfills their needs in language, literacy, and content learning. Activities should be appropriate for children at a variety of Stages of Language Acquisition, with the teacher skillfully modifying whole-class instruction for groups of children with varying English proficiencies. Children need to be invited to use all of their senses in hands-on, meaningful activities instead of hearing an endless, incomprehensible stream of speech.

Developing Children's Oral Language

Characteristics of Classrooms that Support Language Learning

- **Low affective filter** The classroom atmosphere is encouraging and makes children feel comfortable and willing to participate and take risks.

- **Comprehensible input** Supportive strategies make concepts and vocabulary understandable to children at the various Stages of Language Acquisition.

- **Focus on communication** Language is real and is used for authentic, meaningful purposes rather than merely for its own sake.

- **Contextualized language** Context, visuals, examples, and illustrations provide support for integrated oral language, literacy, and content area instruction.

- **Error acceptance** The message, rather than linguistic correctness, is the focus. Errors are corrected through teacher modeling of correct forms rather than drills and exercises.

- **Increased wait time** Adequate time for formulating responses aids in second language production.

- **Respect for Stages of Language Acquisition** Activities chosen are developmentally appropriate for a variety of Stages of Language Acquisition. Language instruction allows learners to stretch their skills and progress to higher Stages.

- **Student-centered activities** Small group and partner activities provide authentic contexts for communication and language use. Student participation and interaction is encouraged. Teacher-talk is kept to a minimum.

- **Use of first language and home culture** When children are allowed to process information with each other in their first language, they maintain self-esteem, build a sense of community, and are able to transfer learning from one language to another. When home culture is used as an asset to classroom instruction, avenues to student participation are opened.

- **Authentic assessment based on multiple measures** Multiple measures, including oral reading records, anecdotal observations, observational checklists, oral language and writing rubrics, and student work samples—when embedded in instruction—provide the teacher with appropriate information for use in planning further instruction.

The Role of Family Members

It is clear from research that the academic and linguistic growth of students is enhanced when collaborative relationships are established between families and school *(Cummins 2000)*. Children who read to family members make significantly greater progress in literacy and English language development even when their parents are neither fluent speakers of English nor literate. Children whose families are involved in their learning show greater interest in learning and behave better in school than those whose families are not involved.

Family involvement in their children's formal education has often been limited to attendance at open houses and report card conferences. Particularly in low-income schools, parents may come from backgrounds of little or no formal education themselves. School may be intimidating for these individuals and conjure up negative emotions and experiences. They may feel inadequate in dealing with school personnel. Also, the relationship between teachers and parents in their home culture might discourage direct parental involvement *(Valdes 1996; Wong-Fillmore 1990)*. Sometimes this gives the mistaken impression that these parents do not care about their children or are not interested in their academic progress. Schools need to explore ways to encourage these parents to become involved in all aspects of their children's education.

Family involvement is more likely when families see the school and classroom as a welcoming environment. The presence of school staff or volunteers who speak their home language will facilitate family involvement. If asked, parents will often bring a trusted friend or family member who can serve as translator to conferences or meetings at school. This puts parents at ease and solves a problem for the staff members who do not speak the parents' language.

Families of English language learners should be regarded as a valuable resource for their own children and for others in school. They need to be empowered to share in policy- and decision-making about their children and the educational community in general. When schools and families work together, students succeed and communities are strengthened.

> *A child's culture operates as a lens through which he or she views the world.*

The Role of Culture

Acquiring a language involves more than simply speaking, reading, and writing the language. It involves thought patterns, perceptions, cultural values, communication styles, and social organizations.

A child's culture operates as a lens through which he or she views the world. Often the culture and language use in the classroom may conflict with what the child has learned in the home culture and language. Sometimes these differences may interfere with student learning or participation in activities. Test performance, group interactions, responses to questioning, homework practices, and learning styles may all be ways in which the culture of the home conflicts with the culture of the classroom. Awareness of these differences will help you deal with them effectively. As students learn English, their success depends on their ability to adapt to the culture of the community. Teachers can facilitate this acculturation process by bridging the culture and language gap for their students. A variety of routines and approaches can help to increase student comfort and success in your classroom. These include valuing the contributions of home languages and cultures, allowing the use of the home language in the classroom when appropriate, encouraging students to make connections to their past experiences and contribute their viewpoints, fostering family involvement in the classroom and in school, and pursuing specific information about the cultures of the students and their families.

Some Myths and Misconceptions About Language Acquisition

There are a number of myths and misconceptions commonly held in today's society regarding second language acquisition. We hope the research-based facts presented here will help you dispel these myths.

Myth: English language learners simply need to be placed in an English learning environment, and they'll pick up English naturally in one year.

Fact: While this approach works well for the acquisition of social English, the acquisition of academic English requires skillful instruction that reaches the child with a limited command of English. Children who receive little or no instruction tailored to the needs of language learners can take as many as ten years to achieve grade level performance in the content areas (Collier 1995).

Myth: If children can already speak English, they don't need any further specialized instruction.

Fact: Even though English language learners may give the impression of being able to speak English well on the playground or with their peers, we know that it typically takes five to seven years for them to acquire grade-level competence in academic subject areas. Integrated instruction in language, literacy, and content can help children acquire academic skills as they learn language. Effective instruction can help reduce this academic gap (Collier 1995).

Developing Children's Oral Language *On Our Way to English*

How Do We Teach Phonological Awareness and Phonics to English Language Learners?

speakers of Arabic may need extensive practice with the *p* sound in English before phonics instruction with the letter *p* since this phoneme does not occur in their language.

To make matters more complex, literacy experiences in the primary language also influence English language learners' response to phonics instruction. English language learners who have had the benefit of literacy instruction in their native language (and whose native language is alphabetic) will be able to transfer much of the information they have acquired about the sound-letter relationships in their primary language to their understanding of reading in English. Research shows that the more developed a child's primary language phonics knowledge is, the more likely he or she is to be able to read words in the new language *(Durgunoglu, et al. 1993)*. Instruction may not be necessary in the sound-symbol relationships that are the same in a child's native language and in English, but rather only those which are new or different in English. For instance, a child who can read and write Spanish may not need instruction for the English letter *n*, which represents the same sound in those languages. On the other hand, a letter that represents two different sounds in the two languages (such as *j*, which is /h/ in Spanish) will require more instruction.

Native speakers of English need exposure to the alphabetic principle and some degree of phonological awareness in order to be ready for phonics instruction. While those are important factors for English language learners as well, an additional key factor is equally crucial: having an understanding of English itself. Phonics in an unknown language is meaningless. For the English language learner, phonological awareness and phonics instruction must make sense and match the child's developmental Stage of Language Acquisition. Therefore, while the teacher must teach these skills explicitly and systematically, he or she also needs to place that instruction in a highly contextualized environment in order for it to be comprehensible to the child. Phonological awareness and phonics instruction must stem from the words and language structures with which children are familiar in order for it to make sense.

For English language learners to understand this instruction, skill words should be in natural contexts and should be semantically related, i.e., *bee*, *busy*, and *buzz*, which have something in common, rather than unrelated words such as *bee*, *boy*, and *bat*. The context stimulates word recognition for the learner.

All of these factors must be considered in the sequencing, pacing, and nature of phonics instruction for English language learners. In *On Our Way to English*, the focus in kindergarten is phonological awareness, letter recognition, and building an awareness of the alphabetic principle, all of which are appropriate for Stages 1 and 2, the language proficiency of the majority of kindergarten language learners. They are not ready for the consonant and vowel instruction of most mainstream kindergarten phonics programs. Following this pace of accessible learning, grade 1 instruction emphasizes consonants and vowels, and grade 2 instruction includes word families, blends, and digraphs. An Enhanced Phonics offering provides an on-grade-level option for second language learners who are ready for this more advanced pacing.

Because children must be able to hear and recognize sounds before they are able to pronounce them, *On Our Way to English* follows the appropriate developmental sequence of recognition, identification, and production of phonics elements through many opportunities to hear, say, sing, chant, rhyme, repeat, and practice. Through this well-developed and sequenced program, English language learners develop phonemic awareness and phonics skills, which will provide a strong foundation for reading achievement in English.

Rigby

On Our Way to English

Grade 2

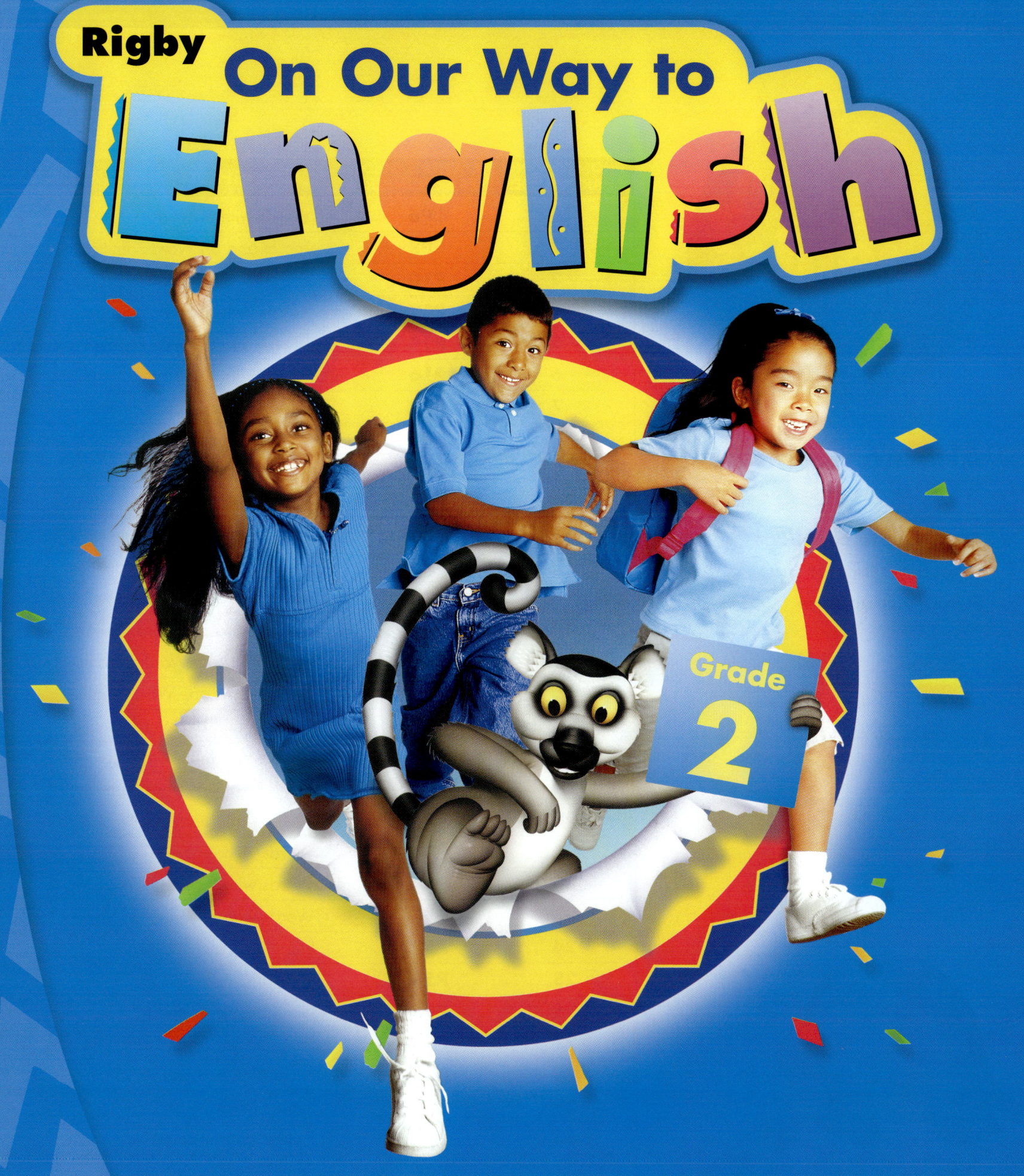

Phonics

Phonics

Alternate Phonics Sequences

According to Language Transfer Issues of the Primary Language

PHONICS SONG CHART NUMBER	TEACHER'S GUIDE PAGE NUMBER	ENGLISH
1	P6	Words with Short *a*
2	P8	The *at* and *an* Word Families
3	P10	The *ag* and *ap* Word Families
4	P12	Words with Short *o*
5	P14	The *op* and *ot* Word Families
6	P16	Words with Short *i*
7	P18	The *ip* and *in* Word Families
8	P20	Words with Short *u*
9	P22	The *un* and *ug* Word Families
10	P24	Words with Short *e*
11	P26	The *et* and *ed* Word Families
12	P28	The *ick* and *ack* Word Families
13	P30	The *ill* and *ell* Word Families
14	P32	The *ake* and *ale* Word Families
15	P34	The *ail* and *ain* Word Families
16	P36	The *oke* and *ope* Word Families
17	P38	The *oad* and *old* Word Families
18	P40	The *ike* and *ide* Word Families
19	P42	The *ie* and *ight* Word Families
20	P44	The *eed* and *eam* Word Families
21	P46	Words with *-y*
22	P48	Words with Long *u* (*uCe*)
23	P50	Words with *R*-Controlled Vowels
24	P52	Initial Blends *cl* and *pl*
25	P54	Initial Blends *sl* and *bl*
26	P56	Initial Blends *gr* and *tr*
27	P58	Initial Blends *br* and *pr*
28	P60	Initial Blends *st* and *sk*
29	P62	Initial Blends *sw* and *sm*
30	P64	Final Blends *-nd* and *-nt*
31	P66	Final Blends *-st* and *-mp*
32	P68	Digraphs *ch* and *sh*
33	P70	Digraphs *th* and *wh*

SPANISH	VIETNAMESE	HMONG
Words with Short o	Words with Short o	Words with Short o
The op and ot Word Families	The op and ot Word Families	The op and ot Word Families
Words with Short a	Words with Short e	Words with Short e
The at and an Word Families	The et and ed Word Families	The et and ed Word Families
The ag and ap Word Families	Words with Short u	Words with Short a
Words with Short i	The un and ug Word Families	The at and an Word Families
The ip and in Word Families	Words with Short a	The ag and ap Word Families
Words with Short u	The at and an Word Families	Words with Short i
The un and ug Word Families	The ag and ap Word Families	The ip and in Word Families
Words with Short e	Words with Short i	Words with Short u
The et and ed Word Families	The ip and in Word Families	The un and ug Word Families
The ick and ack Word Families	The ill and ell Word Families	The ick and ack Word Families
The ill and ell Word Families	The ick and ack Word Families	The ill and ell Word Families
The ake and ale Word Families	The ake and ale Word Families	The eed and eam Word Families
The ail and ain Word Families	The ail and ain Word Families	The ike and ide Word Families
The oke and ope Word Families	The ike and ide Word Families	The ie and ight Word Families
The oad and old Word Families	The ie and ight Word Families	The ake and ale Word Families
The ike and ide Word Families	The eed and eam Word Families	The ail and ain Word Families
The ie and ight Word Families	Words with Long u (uCe)	Words with -y
Words with -y	Words with -y	Words with Long u (uCe)
Words with Long u (uCe)	The oke and ope Word Families	The oke and ope Word Families
The eed and eam Word Families	The oad and old Word Families	The oad and old Word Families
Words with R-Controlled Vowels	Words with R-Controlled Vowels	Words with R-Controlled Vowels
Initial Blends cl and pl	Initial Blends cl and pl	Initial Blends cl and pl
Initial Blends gr and tr	Initial Blends sl and bl	Initial Blends sl and bl
Initial Blends br and pr	Initial Blends gr and tr	Initial Blends st and sk
Final Blends -nd and -nt	Initial Blends br and pr	Initial Blends sw and sm
Final Blends -st and -mp	Initial Blends st and sk	Initial Blends gr and tr
Initial Blends sl and bl	Initial Blends sw and sm	Initial Blends br and pr
Initial Blends st and sk	Final Blends -st and -mp	Final Blends -nd and -nt
Initial Blends sw and sm	Final Blends -nd and -nt	Final Blends -st and -mp
Digraphs ch and sh	Digraphs ch and sh	Digraphs ch and sh
Digraphs th and wh	Digraphs th and wh	Digraphs th and wh

Phonics

Alternate Phonics Sequences

According to Language Transfer Issues of the Primary Language

PHONICS SONG CHART NUMBER	TEACHER'S GUIDE PAGE NUMBER	ENGLISH
1	P6	Words with Short *a*
2	P8	The *at* and *an* Word Families
3	P10	The *ag* and *ap* Word Families
4	P12	Words with Short *o*
5	P14	The *op* and *ot* Word Families
6	P16	Words with Short *i*
7	P18	The *ip* and *in* Word Families
8	P20	Words with Short *u*
9	P22	The *un* and *ug* Word Families
10	P24	Words with Short *e*
11	P26	The *et* and *ed* Word Families
12	P28	The *ick* and *ack* Word Families
13	P30	The *ill* and *ell* Word Families
14	P32	The *ake* and *ale* Word Families
15	P34	The *ail* and *ain* Word Families
16	P36	The *oke* and *ope* Word Families
17	P38	The *oad* and *old* Word Families
18	P40	The *ike* and *ide* Word Families
19	P42	The *ie* and *ight* Word Families
20	P44	The *eed* and *eam* Word Families
21	P46	Words with *-y*
22	P48	Words with Long *u* (*uCe*)
23	P50	Words with *R*-Controlled Vowels
24	P52	Initial Blends *cl* and *pl*
25	P54	Initial Blends *sl* and *bl*
26	P56	Initial Blends *gr* and *tr*
27	P58	Initial Blends *br* and *pr*
28	P60	Initial Blends *st* and *sk*
29	P62	Initial Blends *sw* and *sm*
30	P64	Final Blends *-nd* and *-nt*
31	P66	Final Blends *-st* and *-mp*
32	P68	Digraphs *ch* and *sh*
33	P70	Digraphs *th* and *wh*

CANTONESE	HAITIAN CREOLE
Words with Short *a*	Words with Short *a*
The *at* and *an* Word Families	The *at* and *an* Word Families
The *ag* and *ap* Word Families	The *ag* and *ap* Word Families
Words with Short *o*	Words with Short *e*
The *op* and *ot* Word Families	The *et* and *ed* Word Families
Words with Short *i*	Words with Short *o*
The *ip* and *in* Word Families	The *op* and *ot* Word Families
Words with Short *u*	Words with Short *i*
The *un* and *ug* Word Families	The *ip* and *in* Word Families
Words with Short *e*	Words with Short *u*
The *et* and *ed* Word Families	The *un* and *ug* Word Families
The *ick* and *ack* Word Families	The *ick* and *ack* Word Families
The *ill* and *ell* Word Families	The *ill* and *ell* Word Families
The *ake* and *ale* Word Families	The *ake* and *ale* Word Families
The *ail* and *ain* Word Families	The *ail* and *ain* Word Families
The *oke* and *ope* Word Families	The *oke* and *ope* Word Families
The *oad* and *old* Word Families	The *oad* and *old* Word Families
The *ie* and *ight* Word Families	The *ike* and *ide* Word Families
The *ike* and *ide* Word Families	The *ie* and *ight* Word Families
The *eed* and *eam* Word Families	The *eed* and *eam* Word Families
Words with *-y*	Words with *-y*
Words with Long *u* (*uCe*)	Words with Long *u* (*uCe*)
Words with *R*-Controlled Vowels	Words with *R*-Controlled Vowels
Initial Blends *st* and *sk*	Initial Blends *gr* and *tr*
Initial Blends *sw* and *sm*	Initial Blends *br* and *pr*
Initial Blends *cl* and *pl*	Initial Blends *st* and *sk*
Initial Blends *sl* and *bl*	Initial Blends *sw* and *sm*
Initial Blends *gr* and *tr*	Initial Blends *cl* and *pl*
Initial Blends *br* and *pr*	Initial Blends *sl* and *bl*
Final Blends *-nd* and *-nt*	Final Blends *-nd* and *-nt*
Final Blends *-st* and *-mp*	Final Blends *-st* and *-mp*
Digraphs *ch* and *sh*	Digraphs *ch* and *sh*
Digraphs *th* and *wh*	Digraphs *th* and *wh*

Note: For alphabetic languages, both phonological and orthographic issues have been taken into consideration.

Chart 1

Anna has an apple
for a snack.
She takes it out of her
tan backpack.
Anna has her apple
by her cat.
Anna's black cat
is named Pat.

CHART 1 — Sung to the tune of "I'm a Little Teapot"

Language Junction

The sound of short *a* does not exist in Spanish, so some Spanish-speaking learners of English may find it difficult to hear and produce this sound. Children may produce a sound that is closer to the short *a* in *father* or short *o*. As their English pronunciation becomes more like their native peers, children will be able to perceive the difference naturally.

Words with Short *a*

Setting the Scene

- Bring in several different varieties of apples for a snack, such as golden, green, and red. Pass around the different kinds of apples for the class to explore. Encourage them to compare the sizes, shapes, and colors of the apples. After washing the apples, cut them into bite-sized pieces and invite children to taste each of them. Take a vote to see which kind of apple children like the best.

Creating Comprehensible Input

- Say the chant slowly as you use gestures and pointing to make it comprehensible.

Anna has an apple for a snack.	point to Anna, then to the apple
She takes it out of her tan backpack.	pretend to take something out of a backpack, then point to the backpack
Anna has her apple by her cat.	point to the apple, then point to the cat
Anna's black cat is named Pat.	point to the cat, then point to the word *Pat*

Singing and Gestures

- Invite the class to sing along as you play the song on the Phonics Audio CD. After learning the song, teach children gestures they can make as they sing the song again.
- On the second line of the song, have children pretend they are taking apples out of their backpacks.
- When they sing the word *apple*, have them pretend they are munching on their apples.
- When they sing the word *cat*, have children pretend they are petting their cats.

Recognizing Words with Short *a*

- Sing the first line of the song and point to the word *Anna* as you say it. Write it on the board or easel pad and say the word again. Point to the letter *A* and tell children that the letter *A* stands for the first sound they hear in *Anna*. Ask if they can find any other words that begin with the same sound as the *A* in *Anna*. [*an, apple*] Write these words under the word *Anna*. Point to the word *has* and tell children that the letter *a* stands for the second sound they hear in *has*. Ask if they can find any other words that have the short *a* sound. [*snack, tan, backpack, cat, black, Pat*] Write these words under the word *has*. Ask volunteers for any other easy words they can think of that have /a/. Bear in mind that only children in Stages 3–5 will be able to brainstorm English words based on sounds.
- Invite children to pretend to take a bite out of an apple each time they hear a word that begins with /a/ as you say the following words: *animal, singer, actor, bear, ant, horse, cow, antelope, any, other*.
- Ask children to meow like a cat each time they hear a word that has /a/ in it as you say the following words: *pan, pot, bat, fan, dish, hat, cup, cap, hand, finger*.

STAGES ① Preproduction ② Early Production ③ Speech Emergence ④ Intermediate Fluency ⑤ Advanced Fluency

Exploring Sound-Symbol Relationships

- Locate all of the words that include short *a*. Then use small sticky notes with arrows drawn on them to point to the short *a* in each of these words. This will encourage children to focus on the print of *a*.
- After removing the sticky notes, invite children to come up to the chart page and practice underlining /a/ with their fingers.

Writing Words with Short *a*

- Encourage children to use their phonics skills in writing. Put away the chart page and write the following sentence on the board or easel pad:

    Anna has her _____ by her _____.

- Ask volunteers to tell you what goes in the first blank. Invite the group to say the word *apple* aloud together, stretching the sounds. Count the number of sounds together as you prepare to write them together.
- Ask children to tell you what letter to start *apple* with as you write it down on the board or easel pad. Invite volunteers to come up and write the remaining letters using their phonics skills to match sounds and letters.
- Have children use their own paper to practice writing the letters in the word *apple*.
- Use a similar procedure for the word *cat* in the second blank in the sentence.
- When you are finished, display the chart page and invite children to make comparisons between the words *apple* and *cat* on the chart page and the same words on their own papers. Going back to the original print encourages children to use print resources in their spelling.

Assessment for STAGES

❶❷ Although these children may participate in word family instruction, they should not be expected to master or apply it.

❸ Say the word *apple* and have the child point to the word on the chart page. Identify the letter *a* together and underline it with your finger. Invite him or her to identify which of the following words also begins with short *a*: *spider, ant, worm*. Then say the word *cat* and have the child point to the word on the chart page. Identify the letter *a* together and underline it with your finger. Ask him or her to identify which of the following words has short *a* in it: *fin, fan, fun*.

❹❺ Say the word *apple* and have the child point to the word on the chart page. Ask him or her to identify the letter *a* and underline it with a finger. Have the child think of another word that begins with /a/. Then say the word *cat* and have the child point to the word on the chart page. Ask him or her to identify the letter *a* and underline it with a finger. Ask the child to think of another word that has /a/ in it. If he or she needs help, sing the song together and encourage the child to identify a word in the song.

Take-Home Phonics Story

Reading the Book in Class

- Distribute copies of pages 11–12 from the Take-Home Phonics Stories. Have children create their own books.
- For Emergent readers, read one of the books created by a child to a small group of four to six children one or more times. For Early readers, you can skip this step.
- Invite children to buddy read the book in pairs of heterogeneous stages.
- As they seem ready, have children read the book independently.

Connecting to Home

- Tell children to take the books they made home to share with their families once they are able to read them independently.
- Remember to include the Parent Letter from pages 3–10 of the Take-Home Phonics Stories in the appropriate home language when you send home the book made by each child.

Phonics Song Chart 1   Words with Short *a*   **P7**

CHART 2 — Sung to the tune of "Pawpaw Patch"

Yesterday Dan sat on his tan hat.
Yesterday Dan sat on his red hat.
Yesterday Dan sat on his blue hat.
Now Dan has three flat hats!

Extending to the *am* and *ab* Word Families

Sung to the tune of
"Pawpaw Patch"
Pam saw a crab when she
 swam with her friend Sam.
Pam saw a crab when she
 swam with her friend Sam.
Pam saw a crab when she
 swam with her friend Sam.
They both watched the crab
 grab food to eat!

Language Junction

Words from the *at* and *ad* word families, such as *bat* and *bad*, often sound similar when produced by Cantonese speakers. As a result, Cantonese-speaking children might suggest items from both word families when brainstorming *at* words. These young children will be able to perceive the difference naturally as their English pronunciation becomes more like their peers.

The *at* and *an* Word Families

Setting the Scene

- Bring in hats for children to hold, try on, count, and describe. Include as many different varieties of hats as possible: baseball caps, winter hats, old-fashioned hats, party hats, and so on.
- Invite children to describe their own favorite hats.

Creating Comprehensible Input

- Say the chant slowly as you use gestures and pointing to make it comprehensible.

Yesterday Dan sat on his tan hat.	point to Dan, then to his tan hat
Yesterday Dan sat on his red hat.	point to Dan, then to his red hat
Yesterday Dan sat on his blue hat.	point to Dan, then to his blue hat
Now Dan has three flat hats!	clap hands together vertically as if flattening something

Singing and Gestures

- Play the song on the Phonics Audio CD and sing along with it together. After children have learned the song, teach them gestures they can make as they sing the song.
- As children sing, have them pretend to sit down on hats.
- As they sing the last line, have children straighten their hands flat and put them on top of their heads.

Recognizing the *at* and *an* Word Families

- Sing the first line of the song, then point to the word *Dan* as you say it. Write it on the board or easel pad and say the word again. Point to the letters *an* and tell children that the letters *an* stand for the last two sounds they hear in *Dan*. Ask if they can find another word that sounds like *Dan*. [*tan*] Write the word *tan* under the word *Dan*. Tell children that there are many words that end in /an/. Ask volunteers for any other easy words they can think of that rhyme with *Dan*. Bear in mind that only children in Stages 3–5 will be able to brainstorm English words based on sounds.
- Invite children to put their hands on top of their heads every time they hear /an/ as you say the following words: *pan, pat, man, tin, cap, pet, fan, fat, pot, ran*.
- Repeat the procedure for words that rhyme with *sat*.

Exploring Sound-Symbol Relationships

- Use a small sticky note to cover up the first letter of each word on the chart page that ends with *at* or *an*. This will encourage children to focus on the print of *at* and *an*.
- After removing the sticky notes, invite children to come up to the chart page and practice underlining the letters that make /at/ and /an/ with their fingers.

STAGES ① Preproduction ② Early Production ③ Speech Emergence ④ Intermediate Fluency ⑤ Advanced Fluency

Writing Words from the *at* and *an* Word Families

- Encourage children to use their phonics skills in writing. Put away the chart page and write the following sentence on the board or easel pad:

   Yesterday _____ _____ on his tan hat.

- Ask volunteers to tell you what goes in the first blank. Invite the group to say *Dan* aloud together, stretching the sounds. Count the number of sounds together as you prepare to write them together.
- Ask children to tell you what letter to start *Dan* with as you write it down on the board or easel pad. Invite volunteers to come up and write the remaining letters using their phonics skills to match sounds and letters.
- Have children use their own paper to practice writing the letters in the word *Dan*.
- Use a similar procedure for the word *sat* in the second blank in the sentence.
- When you are finished, display the chart page and invite children to make comparisons between the words *Dan* and *sat* on the chart page and the same words on their own papers. Going back to the original print encourages children to use print resources in their spelling.

Using Word Wall Starters

- **Song Chart Words** Display the words *sat, hat, Dan,* and *tan* from the Word Wall Starters pack. Ask if anyone recognizes the words. Compare the words to *sat, hat, Dan,* and *tan* on the chart page. Invite children to tell you what letters are highlighted in yellow on each card. Use the *short a* label to start the short *a* section of your Word Wall and place the cards *sat, hat, Dan,* and *tan* beneath it, taking care to group word families together. Later as children encounter additional short *a* words in their reading and other class work, write each new word on an index card and highlight the short *a* phonogram. Add these words to this section of your Word Wall as well.

Assessment for STAGES

❶❷ Although these children may participate in word family instruction, they should not be expected to master or apply it.

❸ Say the word *Dan* and have the child point to the word on the chart page. Identify the letters *an* together and underline them with your finger. Invite him or her to identify which of the following words also belongs to the *an* word family: *ball, can, cup.* As desired, use a similar procedure for the *at* word family.

❹❺ Say the word *Dan* and have the child point to the word on the chart page. Ask him or her to identify the letters *an* and underline them with a finger. Have the child think of another word that has /an/ in it. If he or she needs help, sing the song together and encourage the child to identify a word in the song. As desired, use a similar procedure for the *at* word family.

Take-Home Phonics Story

Reading the Book in Class
- Distribute copies of pages 13–14 from the Take-Home Phonics Stories. Have children create their own books.
- For Emergent readers, read one of the books created by a child to a small group of four to six children one or more times. For Early readers, you can skip this step.
- Invite children to buddy read the book in pairs of heterogeneous stages.
- As they seem ready, have children read the book independently.

Word Bank

at		an	
bat	mat	can	pan
cat	pat	Dan	ran
fat	rat	fan	tan
hat	sat	man	van

Connecting to Home
- Tell children to take the books they made home to share with their families once they are able to read them independently.
- Remember to include the Parent Letter from pages 3–10 of the Take-Home Phonics Stories in the appropriate home language when you send home the book made by each child.

Phonics Song Chart 2   The *at* and *an* Word Families

CHART 3

Sung to the tune of "The Farmer in the Dell"

Put on your baseball cap.
Let's wave the flag and clap.
We'll march and we won't
   drag our feet!
Let's wave the flag and clap.

Extending to the ad Word Family

Sung to the tune of "The Farmer in the Dell"
I took a trip with Dad.
The weather wasn't bad.
We both had a lot of fun.
I'm glad I went with Dad!

Language Junction

When /g/ is the last sound in a word, some speakers of Spanish and Korean may tend to substitute /k/. So *tag* may sound more like *tack*. As a result, some Spanish- and Korean-speaking children may need help producing words in word families with the final consonant *g*, or may confuse words ending in /g/ and /k/.

P10

The *ag* and *ap* Word Families

Setting the Scene

- Bring in a variety of baseball caps (or have children use their own) and some small American flags. Explain to children that the flag is a symbol of our country.
- Obtain a CD of patriotic marches from the library. Have children stand in a line and march around the classroom as the music plays. Invite children to put on their baseball caps and either wave their flags or clap to the music.

Creating Comprehensible Input

- Say the chant slowly as you use gestures and pointing to make it comprehensible.

Put on your baseball cap.	point to the baseball cap on the page, then put a real baseball cap on
Let's wave the flag and clap.	point to the flag on the page, then wave a real flag and clap
We'll march and we won't drag our feet!	march, then point to the children's feet on the page
Let's wave the flag and clap.	wave the real flag, then clap

Singing and Gestures

- Play the song on the Phonics Audio CD and sing along with it together. After children have learned the song, teach them gestures they can make as they sing the song.
- As children sing the first line, have them pretend to put on baseball caps.
- On the second line, have children pretend they are waving flags and clapping.
- When children sing the third and fourth lines, have them march to the beat of the music.
- On the last line, have them once again pretend to wave their flags and clap.

Recognizing the *ag* and *ap* Word Families

- Sing the first line of the song, then point to the word *cap* as you say it. Write it on the board or easel pad and say the word again. Point to the letters *ap* and tell children that the letters *ap* stand for the last two sounds they hear in *cap*. Ask if they can find another word that sounds like *cap*. [*clap*] Write the word *clap* under the word *cap*. Tell children that there are many words that end in /ap/. Ask volunteers for any other easy words they can think of that rhyme with *cap*. Bear in mind that only children in Stages 3–5 will be able to brainstorm English words based on sounds.
- Invite children to pretend to put on a baseball cap each time they hear /ap/ as you say the following words: *tap, hop, kick, map, run, lap, nap, sit, flap, gap*.
- Continue the routine for words that rhyme with *flag*.

Exploring Sound-Symbol Relationships

- Use a small sticky note to cover up the first letter of each word on the chart page that ends with *ag* or *ap*. This will encourage children to focus on the print of *ag* or *ap*.
- After removing the sticky notes, invite children to come up to the chart page and practice underlining the letters that make /ap/ and /ag/ with their fingers.

STAGES ① Preproduction ② Early Production ③ Speech Emergence ④ Intermediate Fluency ⑤ Advanced Fluency

Writing Words from the *ag* and *ap* Word Families

- Encourage children to use their phonics skills in writing. Put away the chart page and write the following sentence on the board or easel pad:

  Let's wave the _____ and _____.
- Ask volunteers to tell you what goes in the first blank. Invite the group to say *flag* aloud together, stretching the sounds. Count the number of sounds together as you prepare to write them together.
- Ask children to tell you what letter to start *flag* with as you write it down on the board or easel pad. Invite volunteers to come up and write the remaining letters using their phonics skills to match sounds and letters.
- Have children use their own paper to practice writing the letters in *flag*.
- Use a similar procedure for the word *clap* in the second blank in the sentence.
- When you are finished, display the chart page and invite children to make comparisons between the words *flag* and *clap* on the chart page and the same words on their own papers. Going back to the original print encourages children to use print resources in their spelling.

Using Word Wall Starters

- **Song Chart Words** Display the words *flag*, *drag*, and *cap* from the Word Wall Starters pack. Ask if anyone recognizes the words. Compare the words to *flag*, *drag*, and *cap* on the chart page. Invite children to tell you what letters are highlighted in yellow on each card. Use the *short a* label to start the short *a* section of your Word Wall and place the cards *flag*, *drag*, and *cap* beneath it, taking care to group word families together. Later as children encounter additional short *a* words in their reading and other class work, write each new word on an index card and highlight the short *a* phonogram. Add these words to this section of your Word Wall.
- **Big Book Word** After you have read the Big Book *Hello! I'm Paty*, display the word *clap* from the Word Wall Starters pack. Using the word card and the Big Book, use a procedure similar to the one above, and place the word card *clap* beneath the other *ap* family words.

Assessment for STAGES

❶❷ Although these children may participate in word family instruction, they should not be expected to master or apply it.

❸ Say the word *cap* and have the child point to the word on the chart page. Identify the letters *ap* together and underline them with your finger. Invite him or her to identify which of the following words also belongs to the *ap* word family: *top, map, hip*. As desired, use a similar routine for the *ag* word family.

❹❺ Say the word *cap* and have the child point to the word on the chart page. Ask him or her to identify the letters *ap* and underline them with a finger. Have the child think of another word that has /ap/ in it. If he or she needs help, sing the song together and encourage the child to identify a word in the song. As desired, use a similar routine for the *ag* word family.

Take-Home Phonics Story

Reading the Book in Class
- Distribute copies of pages 15–16 from the Take-Home Phonics Stories. Have children create their own books.
- For Emergent readers, read one of the books created by a child to a small group of four to six children one or more times. For Early readers, you can skip this step.
- Invite children to buddy read the book in pairs of heterogeneous stages.
- As they seem ready, have children read the book independently.

Word Bank

ag		ap	
bag	brag	cap	clap
rag	drag	lap	flap
tag	flag	map	slap
wag	snag	nap	snap
		rap	strap
		sap	trap
		tap	wrap

Connecting to Home

- Tell children to take the books they made home to share with their families once they are able to read them independently.
- Remember to include the Parent Letter from pages 3–10 of the Take-Home Phonics Stories in the appropriate home language when you send home the book made by each child.

Phonics Song Chart 3   The *ag* and *ap* Word Families

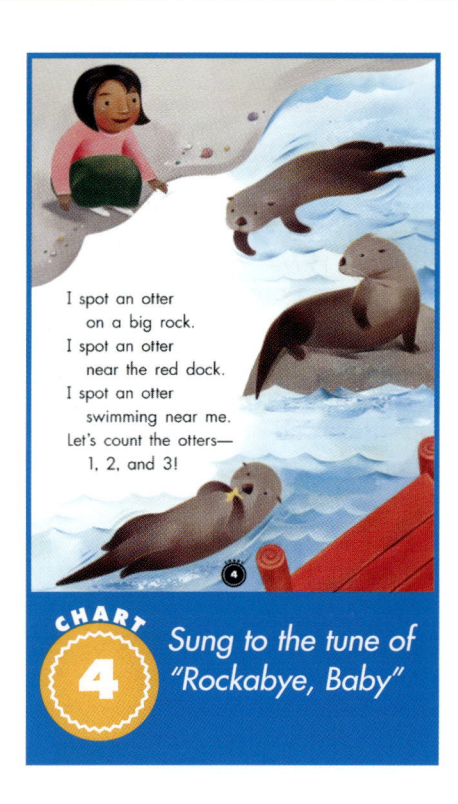

Words with Short o

Setting the Scene

- Bring in a picture of an otter and share it with children. Point out that an otter is an animal with webbed toes, claws, and thick brown fur. Mention that otters live near the water and are very good swimmers.
- Invite children to pretend they are otters swimming in the water.

Creating Comprehensible Input

- Say the chant slowly as you use gestures and pointing to make it comprehensible.

I spot an otter on a big rock.	point to your eye, then to the otter on the big rock
I spot an otter near the red dock.	point to your eye, then to the red dock
I spot an otter swimming near me.	point to your eye, then to the swimming otter
Let's count the otters— 1, 2, and 3!	point to the three otters on the page as you say one, two, three

Singing and Gestures

- Invite the class to sing along as you play the song on the Phonics Audio CD. After they learn the song, teach children gestures to make as they sing the song again.
- Each time children sing the phrase *I spot an otter*, have them point to their eyes, and then pretend they are swimming like otters.
- On the last line of the song, have children hold up the correct number of fingers as they sing *one*, *two*, and *three*.

Recognizing Words with Short o

- Sing the first line of the song and point to the word *otter* as you say it. Write it on the board or easel pad and say the word again. Point to the letter *o* and tell children that the letter *o* stands for the first sound they hear in *otter*. Ask if they can find any other words that begin with the same sound as the *o* in *otter*. [on, otters] Point to the word *spot* and tell children that the letter *o* stands for the middle sound they hear in *spot*. Ask if they can find any other words that have the short *o* sound. [rock, dock] Write the words under the word *spot*. Ask volunteers for any other easy words they can think of that have /o/. Bear in mind that only children in Stages 3–5 will be able to brainstorm English words based on sounds.
- Invite children to pretend to swim like otters each time they hear a word that begins with /o/ as you say the following words: *octopus, paper, omelette, olive, bird, wave, October, at, other, ox*.
- Ask children to pretend to spot an otter each time they hear a word that has /o/ in it as you say the following words: *mat, sock, hot, dig, pot, get, mop, pig, hop, hat*.

CHART 4 — Sung to the tune of "Rockabye, Baby"

I spot an otter on a big rock.
I spot an otter near the red dock.
I spot an otter swimming near me.
Let's count the otters—
1, 2, and 3!

Language Junction

Learners of English from many language backgrounds may have difficulty distinguishing and producing the range of short vowels in English. The sounds of short *o*, short *e*, and short *a* may challenge many learners of English, including speakers of Spanish, Arabic, and Korean. These learners may confuse English short vowel sounds, or produce sounds that resemble long vowels in English.

STAGES: ① Preproduction ② Early Production ③ Speech Emergence ④ Intermediate Fluency ⑤ Advanced Fluency

Exploring Sound-Symbol Relationships

- Locate all of the words that include short *o*. Then use small sticky notes with arrows drawn on them to point to the short *o* in each of these words. This will encourage children to focus on the print of *o*.
- After removing the sticky notes, invite children to come up to the chart page and practice underlining /o/ with their fingers.

Writing Words with Short *o*

- Encourage children to use their phonics skills in writing. Put away the chart page and write the following sentence on the board or easel pad:

    I spot an _____ near the red _____.

- Ask volunteers to tell you what goes in the first blank. Invite the group to say *otter* aloud together, stretching the sounds. Count the number of sounds together as you prepare to write them together.
- Ask children to tell you what letter *otter* starts with as you write it down on the board or easel pad. Invite volunteers to come up and write the remaining letters using their phonics skills to match sounds and letters.
- Have children use their own paper to practice writing the letters in the word *otter*.
- Use a similar procedure for the word *dock* in the second blank in the sentence.
- When you are finished, display the chart page and invite children to make comparisons between the words *otter* and *dock* on the chart page and the same words on their own papers. Going back to the original print encourages children to use print resources in their spelling.

Assessment for STAGES

① ② Although these children may participate in word family instruction, they should not be expected to master or apply it.

③ Say the word *otter* and have the child point to the word on the chart page. Identify the letter *o* together and underline it with your finger. Invite him or her to identify which of the following words also begins with short *o*: *odd, bat, five*. Then say the word *rock* and have the child point to the word on the chart page. Identify the letter *o* together and underline it with your finger. Ask him or her to identify which of the following words has short *o* in it: *win, man, top*.

④ ⑤ Say the word *otter* and have the child point to the word on the chart page. Ask him or her to identify the letter *o* and underline it with a finger. Have the child think of another word that begins with /o/. Then say the word *rock* and have the child point to the word on the chart page. Ask him or her to identify the letter *o* and underline it with a finger. Ask the child to think of another word that has /o/ in it. If he or she needs help, sing the song together and encourage the child to identify a word in the song.

Take-Home Phonics Story

Reading the Book in Class

- Distribute copies of pages 17–18 from the Take-Home Phonics Stories. Have children create their own books.
- For Emergent readers, read one of the books created by a child to a small group of four to six children one or more times. For Early readers, you can skip this step.
- Invite children to buddy read the book in pairs of heterogeneous stages.
- As they seem ready, have children read the book independently.

Connecting to Home

- Tell children to take the books they made home to share with their families once they are able to read them independently.
- Remember to include the Parent Letter from pages 3–10 of the Take-Home Phonics Stories in the appropriate home language when you send home the book made by each child.

The *op* and *ot* Word Families

Setting the Scene

- Make an imaginary vegetable stew with the class. Draw a big pot on the board. Invite children to come up and name a vegetable that they would put into the stew, such as carrots or corn. Then have them draw that vegetable in the pot.
- Invite children to act out making a carrot stew by pretending they are chopping carrots, putting carrots in a pot, and stirring the stew.

Creating Comprehensible Input

- Say the chant slowly as you use gestures and pointing to make it comprehensible.

Let's chop carrots. Chop a lot!	pretend to chop carrots, then point to the carrots
Drop the carrots in a pot.	pretend to drop carrots into a pot
Cook the carrots. Get them hot.	pretend to stir the stew
Let's make a pot of carrot stew.	point to the class, then point to the pot of stew

Singing and Gestures

- Play the song on the Phonics Audio CD and sing along with it together. Teach children gestures they can make after they have learned the song.
- As children sing the first line, have them pretend they are chopping carrots.
- On the second line, have children pretend they are dropping the carrot slices into a pot, one by one.
- When children sing the third line, have them pretend to stir the carrots in the pot.
- On the last line, have children gesture to their classmates to join in.

Recognizing the *op* and *ot* Word Families

- Sing the first line of the song, then point to the word *chop* as you say it. Write it on the board or easel pad and say the word again. Point to the letters *op* and tell children that the letters *op* stand for the last two sounds they hear in *chop*. Ask if they can find another word that sounds like *chop*. [*Drop*] Write the word *Drop* under the word *chop*. Tell children that there are many words that end in /op/. Ask volunteers for any other easy words they can think of that rhyme with *chop*. Bear in mind that only children in Stages 3–5 will be able to brainstorm English words based on sounds.
- Invite children to pretend they are chopping carrots each time they hear /op/ as you say the following words: *run, hop, top, jump, stop, go, mop, sat, drop, bat*.
- Continue the routine for words that rhyme with *lot*.

Exploring Sound-Symbol Relationships

- Use a small sticky note to cover up the first letter of each word on the chart page that ends with *op* or *ot*. This will encourage children to focus on the print of *op* and *ot*.
- After removing the sticky notes, invite children to come up to the chart page and practice underlining the letters that make /op/ and /ot/ with their fingers.

CHART 5

Let's chop carrots. Chop a lot!
Drop the carrots in a pot.
Cook the carrots. Get them hot.
Let's make a pot of carrot stew.

Sung to the tune of "Skip to My Lou"

Extending to the *og* and *ob* Word Family

Sung to the tune of
"Skip to My Lou"
I sit on a log with Bob.
We both eat corn on the cob.
I add butter—one big glob!
Then Bob and I go for a jog.

Language Junction

In Cantonese and Vietnamese, /p/ and /t/ at the end of words are much shorter in length than their English equivalents. As a result, words like *hop* and *hot* may sound like *ha*. Learners may be taught to say the sounds with a puff of air at the end to better approximate the English sound at the end of words. Over time, these children will naturally show an improvement in their pronunciation of these sounds.

STAGES: ① Preproduction ② Early Production ③ Speech Emergence ④ Intermediate Fluency ⑤ Advanced Fluency

Writing Words from the *op* and *ot* Word Families

- Encourage children to use their phonics skills in writing. Put away the chart page and write the following sentence on the board or easel pad:
  _____ the carrots in a _____.
- Ask volunteers to tell you what goes in the first blank. Invite the group to say the word *Drop* together, stretching the sounds. Count the number of sounds together as you prepare to write them together.
- Ask children to tell you what letter *Drop* starts with as you write it down on the board or easel pad. Invite volunteers to come up and write the remaining letters using their phonics skills to match sounds and letters.
- Have children use their own paper to practice writing the letters in the word *Drop*.
- Use a similar procedure for the word *pot* in the second blank in the sentence.
- When you are finished, display the chart page and invite children to make comparisons between the words *Drop* and *pot* on the chart page and the same words on their own papers. Going back to the original print encourages children to use print resources in their spelling.

Using Word Wall Starters

- **Song Chart Words** Display the words *chop*, *drop*, and *pot* from the Word Wall Starters pack. Ask if anyone recognizes the words. Compare the words to *chop*, *Drop*, and *pot* on the chart page. Invite children to tell you what letters are highlighted in yellow on each card. Use the *short o* label to start the short *o* section of your Word Wall and place the cards *chop*, *drop*, and *pot* beneath it, taking care to group word families together. Later as children encounter additional short *o* words in their reading and other class work, write each new word on an index card and highlight the short *o* phonogram. Add these words to this section of your Word Wall as well.
- **Big Book Word** After you have read the Big Book *Hello! I'm Paty*, display the word *hot* from the Word Wall Starters pack. Using the word card and the Big Book, use a procedure similar to the one above, and place the word card *hot* beneath the other *ot* word family words.

Assessment for STAGES

❶❷ Although these children may participate in word family instruction, they should not be expected to master or apply it.

❸ Say the word *chop* and have the child point to the word on the chart page. Identify the letters *op* together and underline them with your finger. Invite him or her to identify which of the following words also belongs to the *op* word family: *shop, fork, miss*. As desired, use a similar routine for the *ot* word family.

❹❺ Say the word *chop* and have the child point to the word on the chart page. Ask him or her to identify the letters *op* and underline them with a finger. Have the child think of another word that has /op/ in it. If he or she needs help, sing the song together and encourage the child to identify a word in the song. As desired, use a similar routine for the *ot* word family.

Take-Home Phonics Story

Reading the Book in Class
- Distribute copies of pages 19–20 from the Take-Home Phonics Stories. Have children create their own books.
- For Emergent readers, read one of the books created by a child to a small group of four to six children one or more times. For Early readers, you can skip this step.
- Invite children to buddy read the book in pairs of heterogeneous stages.
- As they seem ready, have children read the book independently.

Word Bank

op		ot	
bop	crop	cot	rot
hop	drop	dot	tot
mop	flop	got	blot
pop	prop	hot	plot
top	shop	lot	shot
chop	stop	not	spot
		pot	trot

Connecting to Home

- Tell children to take the books they made home to share with their families once they are able to read them independently.
- Remember to include the Parent Letter from pages 3–10 of the Take-Home Phonics Stories in the appropriate home language when you send home the book made by each child.

Phonics Song Chart 5   The *op* and *ot* Word Families

Jin and her twin are both sailors.
They get to go on a ship.
Jin and her twin grin and giggle!
They will have fun on their trip!

CHART 7 Sung to the tune of "My Bonnie Lies Over the Ocean"

Extending to the *im* and *it* Word Families

Sung to the tune of "My Bonnie Lies Over the Ocean"
Jim, Kim, and Tim split a pizza.
They sit and eat by the pool.
Later they swim and play baseball.
It's Sunday! They don't have school!

Language Junction

In some dialects of Spanish, the nasal consonant sounds /m/ and /n/ can be freely substituted for one another at the end of words. As a result, Spanish speakers sometimes confuse these consonants at the ends of English words. So Spanish-speaking learners of English may say *ram* for *ran*, or vice versa. This might cause some confusion if students are asked to work with rhymes that end with these consonants.

The *ip* and *in* Word Families

Setting the Scene

- Bring in a library book about ships. Say the word *ship* and have children echo it after you. Tell children that a ship is a large boat that travels in the ocean or in a very large lake. Show children pictures of ships. Explain to the class that there are many different kinds of ships, such as cruise ships and cargo ships.

Creating Comprehensible Input

- Say the chant slowly as you use gestures and pointing to make it comprehensible.

Jin and her twin are both sailors.	point to the two girls
They get to go on a ship.	point to the ship
Jin and her twin grin and giggle!	pretend you are grinning and giggling
They will have fun on their trip!	point to the two girls

Singing and Gestures

- Play the song on the Phonics Audio CD and sing along with it together. After children have learned the song, teach them gestures they can make as they sing the song.
- As children sing the first line, have them pretend they are putting on sailor hats for their trip.
- On the second line, have children pretend they are marching up a ramp to get on a ship.
- When children sing the third line, have them grin and giggle.
- On the last line, have them pretend to wave good-bye to their friends and family as their ship leaves the dock and heads out to sea!

Recognizing the *ip* and *in* Word Families

- Sing the first line of the song, then point to the word *Jin* as you say it. Write it on the board or easel pad and say the word again. Point to the letters *in* and tell children that the letters *in* stand for the last two sounds they hear in *Jin*. Ask if they can find any other words that sound like *Jin*. [*twin, grin*] Write the words *twin* and *grin* under the word *Jin*. Tell children that there are many words that end with /in/. Ask volunteers for any other easy words they can think of that rhyme with *Jin*. Bear in mind that only children in Stages 3–5 will be able to brainstorm English words based on sounds.
- Invite children to wave good-bye each time they hear /in/ as you say the following words: *pin, fin, look, chin, pop, tin, fall, win, bin, bat*.
- Continue the routine for words that rhyme with *ship*.

Exploring Sound-Symbol Relationships

- Use a small sticky note to cover up the first letter of each word on the chart page that ends with *ip* or *in*. This will encourage children to focus on the print of *ip* and *in*.
- After removing the sticky notes, invite children to come up to the chart page and practice underlining the letters that make /ip/ and /in/ with their fingers.

P18

STAGES ① Preproduction ② Early Production ③ Speech Emergence ④ Intermediate Fluency ⑤ Advanced Fluency

Writing Words from the *ip* and *in* Word Families

- Encourage children to use their phonics skills in writing. Put away the chart page and write the following sentences on the board or easel pad:

  Jin and her _____ are both sailors.

  They get to go on a _____.

- Ask volunteers to tell you what goes in the first blank. Invite the group to say *twin* together, stretching the sounds. Count the number of sounds together as you prepare to write them together.
- Ask children to tell you what letter *twin* starts with as you write it down on the board or easel pad. Invite volunteers to come up and write the remaining letters using their phonics skills to match sounds and letters.
- Have children use their own paper to practice writing the letters in the word *twin*.
- Use a similar procedure for the word *trip* in the second sentence.
- When you are finished, display the chart page and invite children to make comparisons between the words *twin* and *trip* on the chart page and the same words on their own papers. Going back to the original print encourages children to use print resources in their spelling.

Using Word Wall Starters

- **Song Chart Words** Display the words *ship*, *trip*, and *twin* from the Word Wall Starters pack. Ask if anyone recognizes the words. Compare the words to *ship*, *trip*, and *twin* on the chart page. Invite children to tell you what letters are highlighted in yellow on each card. Use the *short i* label to start the short *i* section of your Word Wall and place the cards *ship*, *trip*, and *twin* beneath it, taking care to group word families together. Later as children encounter additional short *i* words in their reading and other class work, write each new word on an index card and highlight the short *i* phonogram. Add these words to this section of your Word Wall as well.
- **Big Book Word** Read the Big Book *Are We There Yet?* Then display the word *chin* from the Word Wall Starters pack. Using the word card and the Big Book, use a procedure similar to the one above, and place the word card *chin* beneath the other *in* word family words.

Assessment for STAGES

❶❷ Although these children may participate in word family instruction, they should not be expected to master or apply it.

❸ Say the word *twin* and have the child point to the word on the chart page. Identify the letters *in* together and underline them with your finger. Invite him or her to identify which of the following words also belongs to the *in* word family: *win*, *tap*, *bat*. As desired, use a similar routine for the *ip* word family.

❹❺ Say the word *twin* and have the child point to the word on the chart page. Ask him or her to identify the letters *in* and underline them with a finger. Have the child think of another word that has /in/. If he or she needs help, sing the song together and encourage the child to identify a word in the song. As desired, use a similar routine for the *ip* word family.

Take-Home Phonics Story

Reading the Book in Class
- Distribute copies of pages 23–24 from the Take-Home Phonics Stories. Have children create their own books.
- For Emergent readers, read one of the books created by a child to a small group of four to six children one or more times. For Early readers, you can skip this step.
- Invite children to buddy read the book in pairs of heterogeneous stages.
- As they seem ready, have children read the book independently.

Word Bank

ip		in	
dip	drip	bin	chin
hip	flip	fin	grin
lip	grip	pin	skin
rip	ship	sin	spin
sip	skip	tin	thin
tip	slip	win	twin
zip	strip		
chip	trip		
clip	whip		

Connecting to Home

- Tell children to take the books they made home to share with their families once they are able to read them independently.
- Remember to include the Parent Letter from pages 3–10 of the Take-Home Phonics Stories in the appropriate home language when you send home the book made by each child.

Phonics Song Chart 7   The *ip* and *in* Word Families

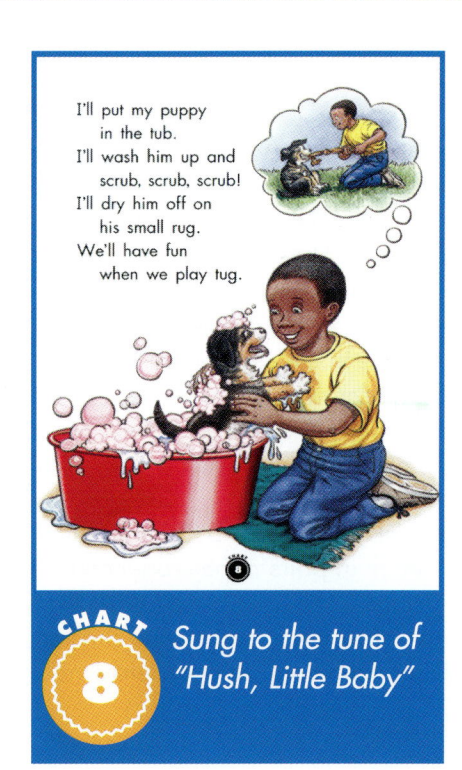

CHART 8 — *Sung to the tune of "Hush, Little Baby"*

> I'll put my puppy
> in the tub.
> I'll wash him up and
> scrub, scrub, scrub!
> I'll dry him off on
> his small rug.
> We'll have fun
> when we play tug.

Language Junction

Because the short *u* sound does not have an equivalent in Korean, children may have difficulty pronouncing it. They may also find it challenging to distinguish it from the other short vowels, particularly from short *o*. Accept approximations for these short vowel sounds at first.

Words with Short *u*

Setting the Scene

- Bring in a book about puppies. Show children pictures of different kinds of puppies. Encourage them to tell you the ways that these puppies are alike and different, such as some have long straight hair, while others have short curly hair. Then have the class vote on their favorite puppy picture.
- Invite children to imagine that they have a puppy for a pet. Have them act out how they would take care of their puppies, such as walking them and feeding them. Ask children to raise their hands if they think that puppies need a lot of love and attention.

Creating Comprehensible Input

- Say the chant slowly as you use gestures and pointing to make it comprehensible.

I'll put my puppy in the tub.	point to the puppy, then point to the tub
I'll wash him up and scrub, scrub, scrub!	pretend to give the puppy a bath
I'll dry him off on his small rug.	pretend to dry off the puppy, then point to the rug
We'll have fun when we play tug.	point to yourself and to the puppy, then pretend to play tug

Singing and Gestures

- Invite the class to sing along as you play the song on the Phonics Audio CD. After learning the song, teach children gestures they can make as they sing the song again.
- Each time children sing *I'll*, have them point to themselves.
- On the second line of the song, have children pretend they are washing and scrubbing their puppies.
- On the third line of the song, have them pretend they are drying off their puppies with towels.
- When they sing the last line, have children pretend they are playing tug with their puppies.

Recognizing Words with Short *u*

- Sing the first line of the song and point to the word *puppy* as you say it. Write it on the board or easel pad and say the word again. Point to the letter *u* and tell children that the letter *u* stands for the second sound they hear in *puppy*. Ask if they can find any other words that have the short *u* sound, including one word that begins with /u/. [*tub, up, scrub, rug, fun, tug*] Write these words under the word *puppy*. Ask volunteers for any other words they can think of that have /u/. Bear in mind that only children in Stages 3–5 will be able to brainstorm English words based on sounds.
- Invite children to pretend they are scrubbing their puppies each time they hear a word that begins with /u/ as you say the following words: *sit, call, umbrella, each, floor, under, upset, into, unzip, tie*.
- Invite children to pretend to play tug with their puppies each time they hear a word that has /u/ in it as you say the following words: *cup, rock, mud, sun, wet, jump, duck, key, tug, hold*.

P20

STAGES ① Preproduction ② Early Production ③ Speech Emergence ④ Intermediate Fluency ⑤ Advanced Fluency

Exploring Sound-Symbol Relationships

- Locate all of the words on the chart page that include short *u*. Then use small sticky notes with arrows drawn on them to point to the short *u* in each of these words. This will encourage children to focus on the print of *u*.
- After removing the sticky notes, invite children to come up to the chart page and practice underlining the letter that makes /u/ in each word with their fingers.

Writing Words with Short *u*

- Encourage children to use their phonics skills in writing. Put away the chart page and write the following sentence on the board or easel pad:

    We'll have _____ when we play _____.

- Ask volunteers to tell you what goes in the first blank. Invite the group to say *fun* aloud together, stretching the sounds. Count the number of sounds together as you prepare to write them together.
- Ask children to tell you what letter *fun* starts with as you write it down on the board or easel pad. Invite volunteers to come up and write the remaining letters using their phonics skills to match sounds and letters.
- Have children use their own paper to practice writing the letters in the word *fun*.
- Use a similar procedure for the word *tug* in the second blank in the sentence.
- When you are finished, display the chart page and invite children to make comparisons between the words *fun* and *tug* on the chart page and the same words on their own papers. Going back to the original print encourages children to use print resources in their spelling.

Assessment for STAGES

❶ ❷ Although these children may participate in word family instruction, they should not be expected to master or apply it.

❸ Say the word *up* and have the child point to the word on the chart page. Identify the letter *u* together and underline it with your finger. Invite him or her to identify which of the following words also begins with short *u*: *coat, umbrella, shoe*. Then say the word *puppy* and have the child point to the word on the chart page. Identify the letter *u* together and underline it with your finger. Invite him or her to identify which of the following words has short *u* in it: *fit, cut, pet*.

❹ ❺ Say the word *up* and have the child point to the word on the chart page. Ask him or her to identify the letter *u* and underline it with a finger. Have the child think of another word that begins with /u/. Then say the word *puppy* and have the child point to the word on the chart page. Ask him or her to identify the letter *u* and underline it with a finger. Ask the child to think of another word that has /u/ in it. If he or she needs additional help, sing the song together and encourage the child to identify a word in the song.

Take-Home Phonics Story

Reading the Book in Class

- Distribute copies of pages 25–26 from the Take-Home Phonics Stories. Have children create their own books.
- For Emergent readers, read one of the books created by a child to a small group of four to six children one or more times. For Early readers, you can skip this step.
- Invite children to buddy read the book in pairs of heterogeneous stages.
- As they seem ready, have children read the book independently.

Connecting to Home

- Tell children to take the books they made home to share with their families once they are able to read them independently.
- Remember to include the Parent Letter from pages 3–10 of the Take-Home Phonics Stories in the appropriate home language when you send home the book made by each child.

Phonics Song Chart 8   Words with Short u

The *un* and *ug* Word Families

Setting the Scene
- Bring in a library book about dogs. Tell children that there are many different breeds, or kinds, of dogs, such as collies, cocker spaniels, and sheep dogs. Show them pictures of these dogs. Tell children that a *pug* is another breed of dog. Show the class a picture of a pug and have children tell you one thing they notice about it.

Creating Comprehensible Input
- As you say the chant slowly, use gestures and pointing to make it comprehensible.

I have fun with my dog, Pug.	point to yourself, then point to the dog, Pug
Pug and I play tug.	point to Pug and then to yourself, then make a tugging motion
Pug and I run in the sun.	point to Pug and then to yourself, then run in place
I give Pug a hug.	point to yourself and to Pug, then make a hugging motion

Singing and Gestures
- Play the song on the Phonics Audio CD and sing along with it together. After children have learned the song, teach them gestures they can make as they sing the song.
- As children sing the first line, have them pretend to pet their dogs.
- On the second line, have children make tugging motions.
- Invite them to run in place as they sing the third line.
- Have children pretend they are hugging their dogs on the last line.

Recognizing the *un* and *ug* Word Families
- Sing the first line of the song, then point to the word *fun* as you say it. Write it on the board or easel pad and say the word again. Point to the letters *un* and tell children that the letters *un* stand for the last two sounds they hear in *fun*. Ask if they can find any other words that sound like *fun*. [run, sun] Write the words *run* and *sun* under the word *fun*. Tell children that there are other words that end in /un/. Ask volunteers for any other easy words they can think of that rhyme with *fun*. Bear in mind that only children in Stages 3–5 will be able to brainstorm English words based on sounds.
- Invite children to run in place each time they hear /un/ as you say the following words: *bun, sit, spun, hop, jump, nun, pun, man, pan, run.*
- Continue the routine for words that rhyme with *Pug*.

Exploring Sound-Symbol Relationships
- Use a small sticky note to cover up the first letter of each word on the chart page that ends with *un* or *ug*. This will encourage children to focus on the print of *un* and *ug*.
- After removing the sticky notes, invite children to come up to the chart page and practice underlining the letters that make /un/ and /ug/ with their fingers.

I have fun with my dog, Pug.
Pug and I play tug.
Pug and I run in the sun.
I give Pug a hug.

CHART 9
Sung to the tune of "Old MacDonald Had a Farm"

Extending to the *up* and *um* Word Family

Sung to the tune of "Old MacDonald Had a Farm"
My pup Buttercup eats a plum.
He barks, "Yum, yum, yum!"
My pup Buttercup eats it up.
What a hungry pup!

Language Junction

Word-final nasal sounds, /n/, /m/, and /ng/, are much shorter in Cantonese than in English. As a result, native English speakers may have difficulty recognizing the nasal sound a Cantonese-speaking learner of English is trying to produce at the end of a word. Cantonese speakers can be taught to lengthen word-final nasal sounds. Over time, these children will naturally show an improvement in their pronunciation of these sounds.

STAGES: 1 Preproduction 2 Early Production 3 Speech Emergence 4 Intermediate Fluency 5 Advanced Fluency

Writing Words from the *un* and *ug* Word Families

- Encourage children to use their phonics skills in writing. Put away the chart page and write the following sentence on the board or easel pad:

    I have _____ with my dog, _____.
- Ask volunteers to tell you what goes in the first blank. Invite the group to say the word *fun* together, stretching the sounds. Count the number of sounds together as you prepare to write them together.
- Ask children to tell you what letter starts *fun* as you write it down on the board or easel pad. Invite volunteers to come up and write the remaining letters using their phonics skills to match sounds and letters.
- Have children use their own paper to practice writing the letters in the word *fun*.
- Use a similar procedure for the word *Pug* in the second blank in the sentence.
- When you are finished, display the chart page and invite children to make comparisons between the words *fun* and *Pug* on the chart page and the same words on their own papers. Going back to the original print encourages children to use print resources in their spelling.

Using Word Wall Starters

- **Song Chart Words** Display the words *run*, *tug*, and *hug* from the Word Wall Starters pack. Ask if anyone recognizes the words. Compare the words to *run*, *tug*, and *hug* on the chart page. Invite children to tell you what letters are highlighted in yellow on each card. Use the *short u* label to start the short *u* section of your Word Wall and place the cards *run*, *tug*, and *hug* beneath it, taking care to group word families together. Later as children encounter additional short *u* words in their reading and other class work, write each new word on an index card and highlight the short *u* phonogram. Add these words to this section of your Word Wall as well.
- **Big Book Word** Read the Big Book *Are We There Yet?* Then display the word *fun* from the Word Wall Starters pack. Using the word card and the Big Book, use a procedure similar to the one above, and place the word card *fun* beneath the other *un* word family words.

Assessment for STAGES

❶❷ Although these children may participate in word family instruction, they should not be expected to master or apply it.

❸ Say the word *fun* and have the child point to the word on the chart page. Identify the letters *un* together and underline them with your finger. Invite him or her to identify which of the following words also belongs to the *un* word family: *cake*, *bun*, *cookie*. As desired, use a similar routine for the *ug* word family.

❹❺ Say the word *fun* and have the child point to the word on the chart page. Ask him or her to identify the letters *un* and underline them with a finger. Have the child think of another word that has /un/ in it. If he or she needs help, sing the song together and encourage the child to identify a word in the song. As desired, use a similar routine for the *ug* word family.

Take-Home Phonics Story

Reading the Book in Class
- Distribute copies of pages 27–28 from the Take-Home Phonics Stories. Have children create their own books.
- For Emergent readers, read one of the books created by a child to a small group of four to six children one or more times. For Early readers, you can skip this step.
- Invite children to buddy read the book in pairs of heterogeneous stages.
- As they seem ready, have children read the book independently.

Word Bank

un		ug	
bun	run	bug	tug
fun	sun	dug	chug
nun	spun	hug	drug
pun	stun	jug	plug
		mug	shrug
		pug	slug
		rug	snug

Connecting to Home
- Tell children to take the books they made home to share with their families once they are able to read them independently.
- Remember to include the Parent Letter from pages 3–10 of the Take-Home Phonics Stories in the appropriate home language when you send home the book made by each child.

Phonics Song Chart 9   The *un* and *ug* Word Families

CHART 10 *Sung to the tune of "Twinkle, Twinkle, Little Star"*

When I woke, I made my bed.
Then I fed my pet named Jed.
Jed likes when we play the best.
Then Jed likes to sit and rest.
When it's time, we go to bed.
I will rest with my pet, Jed.

Language Junction

Distinguishing short *e* and short *a* sounds in English and pronouncing them differently is a particular area of difficulty for Cantonese- and Vietnamese-speaking learners of English. Some of these children may have difficulty producing the short *e* and short *a* sounds in activities using word families. They may confuse words such as *ten* and *tan*.

Words with Short *e*

Setting the Scene

- Invite children to act out what they do when they wake up, such as make their beds, eat breakfast, wash their faces, brush their teeth, and feed their pets.
- Tell children that taking care of a pet is a lot of work. Explain that this work begins early in the morning. For example, we need to feed and walk our pets in the morning. Remind children that pets can be a lot of fun too. Have children imagine that they each have a pet cat. Invite them to show you fun things they could do with their cats throughout the day, such as play with a piece of yarn.

Creating Comprehensible Input

- As you say the chant slowly, use gestures and pointing to make it comprehensible.

When I woke, I made my bed.	rub your eyes, then point to the boy making his bed
Then I fed my pet named Jed.	pretend to hold a dish of cat food, then point to the cat
Jed likes when we play the best.	point to the cat and the boy playing
Then Jed likes to sit and rest.	point to the cat, then sit down
When it's time, we go to bed.	pretend you are falling asleep by placing your head on your hands
I will rest with my pet, Jed.	point to the boy curled up in bed with his cat

Singing and Gestures

- Invite the class to sing along as you play the song on the Phonics Audio CD. After learning the song, teach children gestures they can make as they sing the song again.
- On the first and second lines of the song, have children pretend they are making their beds, then feeding their pet cats.
- On the third line of the song, have them pretend they are playing with their cats.
- On the fourth line of the song, have them sit down and pretend to rest.
- When they sing the last two lines, have children pretend they are falling asleep, curled up with their cats.

Recognizing Words with Short *e*

- Sing the first line of the song and point to the word *When* as you say it. Write it on the board or easel pad and say the word again. Point to the letter *e* and tell children that the letter *e* stands for the middle sound they hear in *When*. Ask if they can find any other words that have the short *e* sound. [*bed, Then, fed, pet, Jed, when, best, rest*]. Write these words under the word *When*. Ask volunteers to think of other words that have /e/, including some that begin with /e/. Bear in mind that only children in Stages 3–5 will be able to brainstorm English words based on sounds.
- Invite children to pretend to make their beds each time they hear a word that begins with /e/ as you say the following words: *every, all, cat, elephant, into, dog, egg, finger, edge, rock*.
- Invite children to pretend to fall asleep each time they hear a word that has /e/ in it as you say the following words: *ten, get, dish, bug, web, hat, red, men, top, sled*.

STAGES ① Preproduction ② Early Production ③ Speech Emergence ④ Intermediate Fluency ⑤ Advanced Fluency

Exploring Sound-Symbol Relationships

- Locate all of the words on the chart page that include short *e*. Then use small sticky notes with arrows drawn on them to point to the short *e* in each of these words. This will encourage children to focus on the print of *e*.
- After removing the sticky notes, invite children to come up to the chart page and practice underlining the letter that makes /e/ in each word with their fingers.

Writing Words with Short e

- Encourage children to use their phonics skills in writing. Put away the chart page and write the following sentence on the board or easel pad:

    Then I _____ my pet named _____.

- Ask volunteers to tell you what goes in the first blank. Invite the group to say *fed* aloud together, stretching the sounds. Count the number of sounds together as you prepare to write them together.
- Ask children to tell you what letter *fed* starts with as you write it down on the board or easel pad. Invite volunteers to come up and write the remaining letters using their phonics skills to match sounds and letters.
- Have children use their own paper to practice writing the letters in the word *fed*.
- Use a similar procedure for the word *Jed* in the second blank in the sentence.
- When you are finished, display the chart page and invite children to make comparisons between the words *fed* and *Jed* on the chart page and the same words on their own papers. Going back to the original print encourages children to use print resources in their spelling.

Assessment for STAGES

❶❷ Although these children may participate in word family instruction, they should not be expected to master or apply it.

❸ Say the word *bed* and have the child point to the word on the chart page. Identify the letter *e* together and underline it with your finger. Invite him or her to identify which of the following words has short *e* in it: *best, sit, tap*. Now say the word *egg*. Invite the child to identify which of the following words also begins with /e/: *sad, play, end*.

❹❺ Say the word *bed* and have the child point to the word on the chart page. Ask him or her to identify the letter *e* and underline it with a finger. Have the child think of another word that has /e/ in it. If he or she needs additional help, sing the song together and encourage the child to identify a word in the song. Now say the word *egg*. Invite the child to think of another word that begins with /e/.

Take-Home Phonics Story

Reading the Book in Class

- Distribute copies of pages 29–30 from the Take-Home Phonics Stories. Have children create their own books.
- For Emergent readers, read one of the books created by a child to a small group of four to six children one or more times. For Early readers, you can skip this step.
- Invite children to buddy read the book in pairs of heterogeneous stages.
- As they seem ready, have children read the book independently.

Connecting to Home

- Tell children to take the books they made home to share with their families once they are able to read them independently.
- Remember to include the Parent Letter from pages 3–10 of the Take-Home Phonics Stories in the appropriate home language when you send home the book made by each child.

The *et* and *ed* Word Families

Setting the Scene

- Show a picture of a sled and say *sled*, inviting children to echo the word. Explain to children that in some parts of the country, it gets very cold and it snows. Mention that children who live in these areas sometimes sit on sleds and slide down snow-covered hills. Ask children if they have ever done this. Encourage them to share their experiences, including what they know about their families' home countries.

Creating Comprehensible Input

- Say the chant slowly as you use gestures and pointing to make it comprehensible.

Ted and Ned go get their sled.	point to the boys, then to the sled
They keep it in the big red shed.	point to the red shed
Ted gets wet and so does Ned,	point to one boy, then to the other
When they fall off their sled!	pretend to fall, then point to the sled

Singing and Gestures

- Play the song on the Phonics Audio CD and sing along with it together. After children have learned the song, teach them gestures they can make as they sing the song.
- As children sing the first line, have them walk in place.
- On the second line, have children make the shape of a roof with their hands.
- As they sing the third line, have them pretend to brush the snow off of themselves.
- On the last line, have children pretend they are falling off their sleds.

Recognizing the *et* and *ed* Word Families

- Sing the first line of the song, then point to the word *Ted* as you say it. Write it on the board or easel pad and say the word again. Point to the letters *ed* and tell children that the letters *ed* stand for the last two sounds they hear in *Ted*. Ask if they can find any other words that sound like *Ted*. [*Ned, sled, red, shed*] Write the words *Ned, sled, red,* and *shed* under the word *Ted*. Tell children that there are many words that end in /ed/. Ask volunteers for any other easy words they can think of that rhyme with *Ted*. Bear in mind that only children in Stages 3–5 will be able to brainstorm English words based on sounds.
- Invite children to pretend they are sitting and holding onto their sleds each time they hear /ed/ as you say the following words: *bed, car, door, fed, led, hair, red, fled, wed, hat*.
- Continue the routine for words that rhyme with *get*.

Exploring Sound-Symbol Relationships

- Use a small sticky note to cover up the first letter of each word on the chart page that ends with *et* or *ed*. This will encourage children to focus on the print of *et* and *ed*.
- After removing the sticky notes, invite children to come up to the chart page and practice underlining the letters that make /et/ and /ed/ with their fingers.

CHART 11 *Sung to the tune of "The Muffin Man"*

Ted and Ned go get their sled.
They keep it in the big red shed.
Ted gets wet and so does Ned,
When they fall off their sled!

Extending to the *en* Word Family

Sung to the tune of
 "The Muffin Man"
Jen and Ben sit in the den.
They babysit their brother Ken.
They teach Ken how to count
 to ten.
Then they play a game!

Language Junction

When /d/ is the last sound in a word, many Spanish speakers tend to make /d/ sound like /t/. So the word *bed* may sound more like *bet*. Speakers of Tagalog and Cantonese may tend to have the same problem. As a result, it may be hard for an English speaker to distinguish between sets of words that differ only by the final /t/ or /d/ when said by speakers of these languages.

STAGES ① Preproduction ② Early Production ③ Speech Emergence ④ Intermediate Fluency ⑤ Advanced Fluency

Writing Words from the *et* and *ed* Word Families

- Encourage children to use their phonics skills in writing. Put away the chart page and write the following sentence on the board or easel pad:

    Ted and Ned go _____ their _____.

- Ask volunteers to tell you what goes in the first blank. Invite the group to say *get* together, stretching the sounds. Count the number of sounds together as you prepare to write them together.
- Ask children to tell you what letter to start *get* with as you write it down on the board or easel pad. Invite volunteers to come up and write the remaining letters using their phonics skills to match sounds and letters.
- Have children use their own paper to practice writing the letters in the word *get*.
- Use a similar procedure for the word *sled* in the second blank in the sentence.
- When you are finished, display the chart page and invite children to make comparisons between the words *get* and *sled* on the chart page and the same words on their own papers. Going back to the original print encourages children to use print resources in their spelling.

Using Word Wall Starters

- **Song Chart Words** Display the words *wet*, *sled*, and *shed* from the Word Wall Starters pack. Ask if anyone recognizes the words. Compare the words to *wet*, *sled*, and *shed* on the chart page. Invite children to tell you what letters are highlighted in yellow on each card. Use the *short e* label to start the short *e* section of your Word Wall and place the cards *wet*, *sled*, and *shed* beneath it, taking care to group word families together. Later as children encounter additional short *e* words in their reading and other class work, write each new word on an index card and highlight the short *e* phonogram. Add these words to this section of your Word Wall as well.
- **Big Book Word** After you have read the Big Book *A Pocketful of Opossums*, display the word *get* from the Word Wall Starters pack. Using the word card and the Big Book, use a procedure similar to the one above, and place the word card *get* beneath the other *et* word family cards.

Assessment for STAGES

❶❷ Although these children may participate in word family instruction, they should not be expected to master or apply it.

❸ Say the word *Ted* and have the child point to the word on the chart page. Identify the letters *ed* together and underline them with your finger. Invite him or her to identify which of the following words also belongs to the *ed* word family: *chair, bed, table*. As desired, use a similar routine for the *et* word family.

❹❺ Say the word *Ned* and have the child point to the word on the chart page. Ask him or her to identify the letters *ed* and underline them with a finger. Have the child think of another word that has /ed/ in it. If he or she needs help, sing the song together and encourage the child to identify a word in the song. As desired, use a similar routine for the *et* word family.

Take-Home Phonics Story

Reading the Book in Class

- Distribute copies of pages 31–32 from the Take-Home Phonics Stories. Have children create their own books.
- For Emergent readers, read one of the books created by a child to a small group of four to six children one or more times. For Early readers, you can skip this step.
- Invite children to buddy read the book in pairs of heterogeneous stages.
- As they seem ready, have children read the book independently.

Word Bank

et		ed	
bet	net	bed	wed
get	pet	fed	fled
jet	set	Jed	Fred
let	wet	led	shed
met	yet	Ned	shred
		red	sled
		Ted	sped

Connecting to Home

- Tell children to take the books they made home to share with their families once they are able to read them independently.
- Remember to include the Parent Letter from pages 3–10 of the Take-Home Phonics Stories in the appropriate home language when you send home the book made by each child.

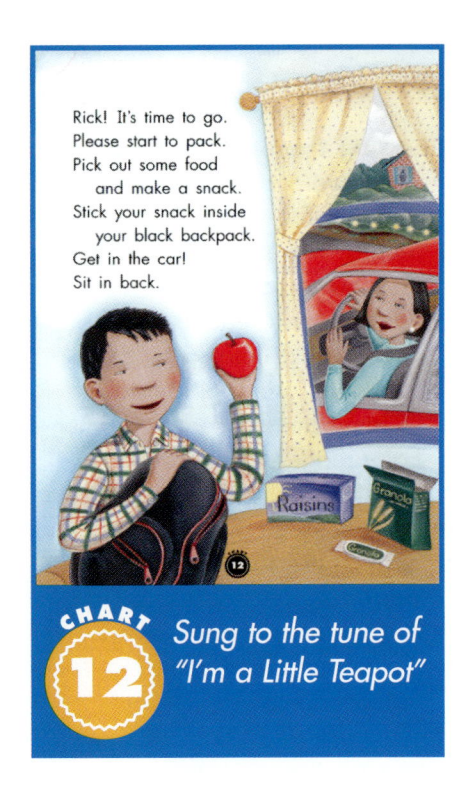

Rick! It's time to go.
Please start to pack.
Pick out some food
   and make a snack.
Stick your snack inside
   your black backpack.
Get in the car!
Sit in back.

CHART 12 — Sung to the tune of "I'm a Little Teapot"

Language Junction

Very few words in Spanish end with /k/, but many end with /k/ followed by a vowel. So children whose home language is Spanish may tend to add an additional sound after /k/. As a result, they may need extra practice with words ending in *ck*.

The *ick* and *ack* Word Families

Setting the Scene

- Bring in sliced apples, granola, and raisins. Allow each child to try these healthy snacks. Encourage children to name other healthy snacks they like to eat.

Creating Comprehensible Input

- Say the chant slowly as you use gestures and pointing to make it comprehensible.

Rick! It's time to go.	point to Rick, then point to your watch
Please start to pack.	act out putting items into the backpack
Pick out some food and make a snack.	point to the snacks
Stick your snack inside your black backpack.	point to the backpack
Get in the car!	point to the car
Sit in back.	point to the backseat of the car

Singing and Gestures

- Play the song on the Phonics Audio CD and sing along with it together. After children have learned the song, teach them gestures they can make as they sing the song.
- As children sing the first line of the song, have them beckon to someone.
- As they continue singing, invite children to pretend they are picking out snack foods and making a snack, such as a peanut butter and jelly sandwich. Then have them pretend to unzip their backpack, place the snack inside, then zip up the backpack.
- On the last two lines of the song, have children pretend they are opening a car door, getting inside, sitting down, and then shutting the door.

Recognizing the *ick* and *ack* Word Families

- Sing the first line of the song, then point to the word *Rick* as you say it. Write it on the board or easel pad and say the word again. Point to the letters *ick* and tell children that the letters *ick* stand for the last two sounds they hear in *Rick*, even though there are three letters. Ask if they can find any other words that sound like *Rick*. [*Pick, Stick*] Write the words *Pick* and *Stick* under the word *Rick*. Tell children that there are many words that end in /ick/. Ask volunteers for any other easy words they can think of that rhyme with *Rick*. Bear in mind that only children in Stages 3–5 will be able to brainstorm English words based on sounds.
- Invite children to beckon to someone each time they hear /ick/ as you say the following words: *stick, door, lick, brick, stone, rock, kick, trick, hit, tick*.
- Continue the routine for words that rhyme with *pack*.

Exploring Sound-Symbol Relationships

- Use a small sticky note to cover up the first letter of each word on the chart page that ends with *ick* or *ack*. This will encourage children to focus on the print.
- After removing the sticky notes, invite children to come up to the chart page and practice underlining the letters that make /ick/ and /ack/ with their fingers.

STAGES ① Preproduction ② Early Production ③ Speech Emergence ④ Intermediate Fluency ⑤ Advanced Fluency

Writing Words from the *ick* and *ack* Word Families

- Encourage children to use their phonics skills in writing. Put away the chart page and write the following sentence on the board or easel pad:
  _____ *out some food and make a* _____.
- Ask volunteers to tell you what goes in the first blank. Invite the group to say the word *Pick* together, stretching the sounds.
- Ask children to tell you what letter to start *Pick* with as you write it down on the board or easel pad. Invite volunteers to come up and write the remaining letters using their phonics skills to match sounds and letters.
- Have children use their own paper to practice writing the letters in the word *Pick*.
- Use a similar procedure for the word *snack* in the second blank in the sentence.
- When you are finished, display the chart page and invite children to make comparisons between the words *Pick* and *snack* on the chart page and the same words on their own papers. Going back to the original print encourages children to use print resources in their spelling.

Using Word Wall Starters

- **Song Chart Word** Display the word *pick* from the Word Wall Starters pack. Ask if anyone recognizes the word. Compare the word to *Pick* on the chart page. Invite children to tell you what letters are highlighted in yellow on the card. Use the -*ck* label to start the *ck* section of your Word Wall and place the card *pick* beneath it. Later as children encounter additional words that end with *ck* in their reading and other class work, write each new word on an index card and highlight the *ck*. Add these words to this section of your Word Wall as well.
- **Big Book Word** After you have read the Big Book *A Pocketful of Opossums*, display the word *back* from the Word Wall Starters pack. Using the word card and the Big Book, use a routine similar to the one above, and place the word card *back* beneath the other *ck* word cards.

Assessment for STAGES

❶❷ Although these children may participate in word family instruction, they should not be expected to master or apply it.

❸ Say the word *Rick* and have the child point to the word on the chart page. Identify the letters *ick* together and underline them with your finger. Invite him or her to identify which of the following words also belongs to the *ick* word family: *wood, log, stick*. As desired, use a similar routine for the *ack* word family.

❹❺ Say the word *Rick* and have the child point to the word on the chart page. Ask him or her to identify the letters *ick* and underline them with a finger. Have the child think of another word that has /ick/ in it. If he or she needs help, sing the song together and encourage the child to identify a word in the song. As desired, use a similar routine for the *ack* word family.

Take-Home Phonics Story

Reading the Book in Class

- Distribute copies of pages 33–34 from the Take-Home Phonics Stories. Have children create their own books.
- For Emergent readers, read one of the books created by a child to a small group of four to six children one or more times. For Early readers, you can skip this step.
- Invite children to buddy read the book in pairs of heterogeneous stages.
- As they seem ready, have children read the book independently.

Word Bank

ick		ack	
Dick	wick	back	black
kick	brick	Jack	crack
lick	chick	lack	shack
Nick	click	Mack	slack
pick	flick	pack	smack
quick	slick	quack	snack
Rick	stick	rack	stack
sick	thick	sack	track
tick	trick	tack	whack

Connecting to Home

- Once children are able to read their books independently, invite them to take the books home to share with their families.
- Remember to include the Parent Letter from pages 3–10 of the Take-Home Phonics Stories in the appropriate home language when you send home the book made by each child.

Phonics Song Chart 12   The *ick* and *ack* Word Families   **P29**

> Jill doesn't feel well.
> I sure can tell!
> I am her sister.
> My name is Nell.
> I will help Jill
> because she is ill.
> Here is a blanket.
> Don't catch a chill!

CHART 13 — Sung to the tune of "Rockabye, Baby"

The *ill* and *ell* Word Families

Setting the Scene

- Bring in a blanket, thermometer, and box of tissues to class. Tell children that these items are sometimes needed when someone is not feeling well. Ask children to think about a time when they used these things. Encourage them to share their experiences.

Creating Comprehensible Input

- Say the chant slowly as you use gestures and pointing to make it comprehensible.

Jill doesn't feel well.	point to Jill in the bed
I sure can tell!	nod your head
I am her sister.	point to the other girl
My name is Nell.	point to the word *Nell* on the page
I will help Jill because she is ill.	point to Jill, then act out feeling ill
Here is a blanket.	point to the blanket
Don't catch a chill!	hold your arms and rub them as if you are cold

Singing and Gestures

- Play the song on the Phonics Audio CD and sing along with it together. Teach children gestures they can make once they learn the song.
- As children sing the first line, invite them to pretend they have a chill.
- Each time children sing the word *I*, have them point to themselves.
- As they sing the last two lines, invite children to pretend they are covering Jill with a blanket.

Recognizing the *ill* and *ell* Word Families

- Sing the first line of the song, then point to the word *Jill* as you say it. Write it on the board or easel pad and say the word again. Point to the letters *ill* and tell children that the letters *ill* stand for the last two sounds they hear in *Jill*, even though there are three letters. Ask if they can find any other words that sound like *Jill*. [*will, ill, chill*] Write the words *will, ill,* and *chill* under the word *Jill*. Tell children that there are many words that end in /ill/. Ask volunteers for any other easy words they can think of that rhyme with *Jill*. Bear in mind that only children in Stages 3–5 will be able to brainstorm English words based on sounds.
- Invite children to pretend they have a chill each time they hear /ill/ as you say the following words: *bill, ball, kick, fill, hill, lake, mill, pill, wall, grill.*
- Continue the routine for words that rhyme with *tell.*

Exploring Sound-Symbol Relationships

- Use a small sticky note to cover up the first letter of each word on the chart page that ends in *ill* or *ell*. This will encourage children to focus on the print of *ill* and *ell*.
- After removing the sticky notes, invite children to come up to the chart page and practice underlining the letters that make /ill/ and /ell/ with their fingers.

Language Junction

Some Cantonese learners of English tend to produce a sound more like /w/ than the English /l/ at the end of words such as *call*. So a word such as *call* may sound like *caw*. This can result in difficulties in comprehension. A tip for pronunciation of English /l/ is to ask learners to say long *o* with their tongues touching the top of their front teeth and their lips not rounded.

STAGES: ① Preproduction ② Early Production ③ Speech Emergence ④ Intermediate Fluency ⑤ Advanced Fluency

Writing Words from the *ill* and *ell* Word Families

- Encourage children to use their phonics skills in writing. Put away the chart page and write the following sentence on the board or easel pad:
  _____ *doesn't feel* _____.
- Ask volunteers to tell you what goes in the first blank. Invite the group to say the word *Jill* together, stretching the sounds.
- Ask children to tell you what letter to start *Jill* with as you write it down on the board or easel pad. Invite volunteers to come up and write the remaining letters using their phonics skills to match sounds and letters.
- Have children use their own paper to practice writing the letters in the word *Jill*.
- Use a similar procedure for the word *well* in the second blank in the sentence.
- When you are finished, display the chart page and invite children to make comparisons between the words *Jill* and *well* on the chart page and the same words on their own papers. Going back to the original print encourages children to use print resources in their spelling.

Using Word Wall Starters

- **Song Chart Word** Display the word *tell* from the Word Wall Starters pack. Ask if anyone recognizes the word. Compare the word to *tell* on the chart page. Invite children to tell you what letters are highlighted in yellow on the card. Use the -*ll* label to start the *ll* section of your Word Wall and place the card *tell* beneath it. Later as children encounter additional words that end with *ll* in their reading and other class work, write each new word on an index card and highlight the *ll*. Add these words to this section of your Word Wall as well.
- **Big Book Word** After you have read the Big Book *A Pocketful of Opossums*, display the word *will* from the Word Wall Starters pack. Using the word card and the Big Book, use a routine similar to the one above, and place the card *will* beneath the other *ll* word cards.

Assessment for STAGES

❶❷ Although these children may participate in word family instruction, they should not be expected to master or apply it.

❸ Say the word *Jill* and have the child point to the word on the chart page. Identify the letters *ill* together and underline them with your finger. Invite him or her to identify which of the following words also belongs to the *ill* word family: *fill, get, top*. As desired, use a similar routine for the *ell* word family.

❹❺ Say the word *Jill* and have the child point to the word on the chart page. Ask him or her to identify the letters *ill* and underline them with a finger. Have the child think of another word that has /ill/ in it. If he or she needs help, sing the song together and encourage the child to identify a word in the song. As desired, use a similar routine for the *ell* word family.

Take-Home Phonics Story

Reading the Book in Class

- Distribute copies of pages 35–36 from the Take-Home Phonics Stories. Have children create their own books.
- For Emergent readers, read one of the books created by a child to a small group of four to six children one or more times. For Early readers, you can skip this step.
- Invite children to buddy read the book in pairs of heterogeneous stages.
- As they seem ready, have children read the book independently.

Word Bank

ill		ell	
bill	sill	bell	well
dill	till	cell	yell
fill	will	fell	dwell
gill	chill	Nell	shell
hill	drill	sell	smell
ill	grill	tell	spell
Jill	skill		swell
mill	spill		
pill	still		
	thrill		

Connecting to Home

- Tell children to take the books they made home to share with their families once they are able to read them independently.
- Be sure to include the Parent Letter from pages 3–10 of the Take-Home Phonics Stories in the appropriate home language when you send home the book made by each child.

My bake sale! My bake sale!
Come to my first bake sale.
Come and try the treats I make.
You can take a piece of cake.
My bake sale! My bake sale!
Come to my first bake sale.
I'll weigh the cookies on my scale.
Nothing that I sell is stale!

CHART 14
Sung to the tune of "A Tisket, a Tasket"

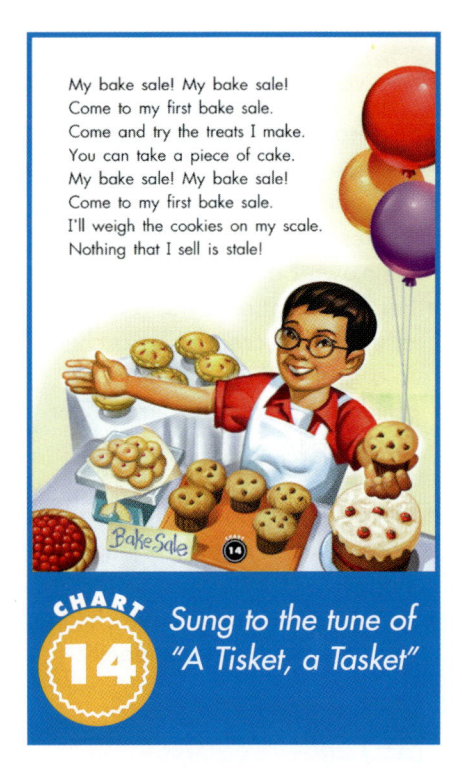

Extending to the *ame* and *ate* Word Families

Sung to the tune of "A Tisket, a Tasket"
Kate came home. Kate came home.
Kate, my kitten, came home.
Last night when it was so late,
 Kate ran out the garden gate.
Kate came home. Kate came home.
Kate, my kitten, came home.
When I called Kate's name today,
 Kate came running in to play!

Language Junction

In Spanish, the vowels *a, e, i, o,* and *u* each stand for one sound. Therefore, Spanish-speaking learners of English may have difficulty with the concept that the letter *a* can stand for both short and long vowel sounds. In addition, they may need to practice distinguishing and pronouncing short *a* and long *a*.

P32

The *ake* and *ale* Word Families

Setting the Scene
- Have children draw bake sale items and display their pictures on a table. Have children take turns pretending to buy and sell the baked goods.

Creating Comprehensible Input
- Say the chant slowly as you use gestures and pointing to make it comprehensible.

My bake sale. My bake sale.	point to the sign that says *Bake Sale*
Come to my first bake sale.	make a motion that indicates *come*, then point to the sign
Come and try the treats I make.	make a motion that indicates *come*, then point to the treats on the table
You can take a piece of cake.	point to the class, then point to the cake
My bake sale. My bake sale.	point to the sign
Come to my first bake sale.	make a motion that indicates *come*, then point to the sign
I'll weigh the cookies on my scale.	point to the cookies, then point to the scale
Nothing that I sell is stale!	shake your head *no*

Singing and Gestures
- Sing the song together as you play it on the Phonics Audio CD.
- Each time children sing the words *my, I,* and *I'll,* have them point to themselves.
- Each time children sing the word *come,* have them motion to a friend to come.

Recognizing the *ake* and *ale* Word Families
- Sing the first line of the song, then point to the word *bake* as you say it. Write it on the board or easel pad and say the word again. Point to the letters *ake* and tell children that the letters *ake* stand for the last two sounds they hear in *bake,* even though there are three letters. Ask if they can find any other words that sound like *bake.* [make, cake] Write these words under the word *bake.* Ask volunteers for any other words they can think of that rhyme with *bake.* Bear in mind that only children in Stages 3–5 will be able to brainstorm English words based on sounds.
- Invite children to pretend they are eating a piece of cake each time they hear the *ake* sound as in *bake* as you say the following words: *fake, fall, wake, lake, river, walk, take, bear, rock, rake.*
- Continue this routine for words that rhyme with *sale.*

Exploring Sound-Symbol Relationships
- Use a small sticky note to cover up the first letter or letters of each word on the chart page that ends with *ake* or *ale.* This will encourage children to focus on the print of *ake* and *ale.*
- After removing the sticky notes, invite children to come up to the chart page and practice underlining the letters that make the *ake* sound as in *bake* and the *ale* sound as in *sale* with their fingers.

STAGES ① Preproduction ② Early Production ③ Speech Emergence ④ Intermediate Fluency ⑤ Advanced Fluency

Writing Words from the *ake* and *ale* Word Families

- Encourage children to use their phonics skills in writing. Put away the chart page and write the following sentence on the board or easel pad:
  Come to my first _____ _____.
- Ask volunteers to tell you what goes in the first blank. Invite the group to say the word *bake* together, stretching the sounds.
- Ask children to tell you what letter to start *bake* with as you write it down on the board or easel pad. Invite volunteers to come up and write the remaining letters using their phonics skills to match sounds and letters.
- Have children use their own paper to practice writing the letters in the word *bake*.
- Use a similar procedure for the word *sale* in the second blank in the sentence.
- When you are finished, display the chart page and invite children to make comparisons between the words *bake* and *sale* on the chart page and the same words on their own papers. Going back to the original print encourages children to use print resources in their spelling.

Using Word Wall Starters

- **Song Chart Words** Display the words *bake*, *sale*, and *scale* from the Word Wall Starters pack. Ask if anyone recognizes the words. Compare the words to *bake*, *sale*, and *scale* on the chart page. Invite children to tell you what letters are highlighted in yellow on each card. Use the *long a* label to start the long *a* section of your Word Wall and place the cards *bake*, *sale*, and *scale* beneath it, taking care to group word families together. Later as children encounter additional long *a* words in their reading and other class work, write each new word on an index card and highlight the long *a* phonogram. Add these words to this section of your Word Wall.
- **Big Book Word** After you have read the Big Book *What Fine Gardeners*, display the word *rake* from the Word Wall Starters pack. Using the word card and the Big Book, use a routine similar to the one above, and place the word card *rake* beneath the other *ake* word family words.

Assessment for STAGES

❶❷ Although these children may participate in word family instruction, they should not be expected to master or apply it.

❸ Say the word *bake* and have the child point to the word on the chart page. Identify the letters *ake* together and underline them with your finger. Invite him or her to identify which of the following words also belongs to the *ake* word family: *take, give, hand*. As desired, use a similar routine for the *ale* word family.

❹❺ Say the word *bake* and have the child point to the word on the chart page. Ask him or her to identify the letters *ake* and underline them with a finger. Have the child think of another word that has the sound *ake* as in *bake* in it. If he or she needs additional help, sing the song together and encourage the child to identify a word in the song. As desired, use a similar routine for the *ale* word family.

Take-Home Phonics Story

Reading the Book in Class
- Distribute copies of pages 37–38 from the Take-Home Phonics Stories. Have children create their own books.
- For Emergent readers, read one of the books created by a child to a small group of four to six children one or more times. For Early readers, you can skip this step.
- Invite children to buddy read the book in pairs of heterogeneous stages.
- As they seem ready, have children read the book independently.

Word Bank

ake		ale	
bake	take	bale	tale
cake	wake	male	scale
fake	brake	pale	stale
Jake	drake	sale	whale
lake	flake		
make	shake		
quake	snake		
rake	stake		

Connecting to Home

- Tell children to take the books they made home to share with their families once they are able to read them independently.
- Be sure to include the Parent Letter from pages 3–10 of the Take-Home Phonics Stories in the appropriate home language when you send home the book made by each child.

Phonics Song Chart 14   *The ake and ale Word Families*

The *ail* and *ain* Word Families

Setting the Scene

- Bring in different kinds of berries, such as strawberries, blueberries, raspberries, and blackberries. Invite children to taste each kind. Ask children if they have ever tasted these kinds of berries before. Encourage volunteers to share their experiences with these fruits.

Creating Comprehensible Input

- Say the chant slowly as you use gestures and pointing to make it comprehensible.

Gail was walking on a trail when suddenly she felt rain.	walk in place, then hold your hands out and look up at the sky
She turned to go but dropped her pail.	turn around, then point to the pail
She fell and got a mud stain.	pretend you are falling, then point to the mud stain on Gail's pants

Singing and Gestures

- Sing the song together as you play it on the Phonics Audio CD. Once they learn the song, teach children gestures they can make to go along with it.
- Invite children to walk around the room as they sing. When they sing the word *rain*, have them hold their hands out to pretend to feel the raindrops.
- On the second line, have them turn around and pretend to drop their pails.
- As children sing the last line, have them pretend to fall.

Recognizing the *ail* and *ain* Word Families

- Sing the first line of the song, then point to the word *Gail* as you say it. Write it on the board or easel pad and say the word again. Point to the letters *ail* and tell children that the letters *ail* stand for the ending sounds they hear in *Gail*. Ask if they can find any other words that sound like *Gail*. [*trail*, *pail*] Write these words under the word *Gail*. Tell children that there are many words that end in the *ail* sound as in *Gail*. Ask volunteers for any other words they can think of that rhyme with *Gail*. Bear in mind that only children in Stages 3–5 will be able to brainstorm English words based on sounds.
- Invite children to pretend to reach into a pail each time they hear the *ail* sound as in *Gail* as you say the following words: *fail, fall, hail, money, mail, sail, penny, nail, leg, tail*.
- Continue in a similar manner for words that rhyme with *rain*.

Exploring Sound-Symbol Relationships

- Use a small sticky note to cover up the first letter or letters of each word on the chart page that ends with *ail* or *ain*. This will encourage children to focus on the print of *ail* and *ain*.
- After removing the sticky notes, invite children to come up to the chart page and practice underlining the letters that make the *ail* sound as in *Gail* and the *ain* sound as in *rain* with their fingers.

CHART 15

Gail was walking on a trail
when suddenly she felt rain.
She turned to go but dropped her pail.
She fell and got a mud stain.

Sung to the tune of "Yankee Doodle"

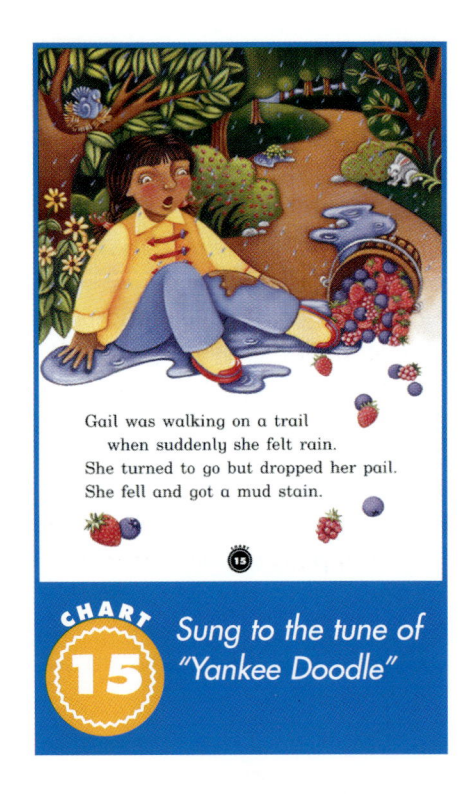

Extending to the *ay* Word Family

Sung to the tune of "Yankee Doodle"
I will stay inside today.
It is a rainy Sunday.
I may play a game or two.
I hope the rain stops Monday!

Language Junction

The Hmong language does not have a long *a* sound, so Hmong-speaking children may have difficulty producing the long *a* sound at first. An even more difficult challenge may be spelling. Children familiar with Hmong print may decode *ai* as long *i* since the letters *ai* stand for that sound in written Hmong.

P34

STAGES ① Preproduction ② Early Production ③ Speech Emergence ④ Intermediate Fluency ⑤ Advanced Fluency

Writing Words from the *ail* and *ain* Word Families

- Encourage children to use their phonics skills in writing. Put away the chart page and write the following sentence on the board or easel pad:

    Gail was walking on a _____ when suddenly she felt _____.

- Ask volunteers to tell you what goes in the first blank. Invite the group to say the word *trail* together, stretching the sounds.
- Ask children to tell you what letter to start *trail* with as you write it down on the board or easel pad. Invite volunteers to come up and write the remaining letters using their phonics skills to match sounds and letters.
- Have children use their own paper to practice writing the letters in the word *trail*.
- Use a similar procedure for the word *rain* in the second blank in the sentence.
- When you are finished, display the chart page and invite children to make comparisons between the words *trail* and *rain* on the chart page and the same words on their own papers. Going back to the original print encourages children to use print resources in their spelling.

Using Word Wall Starters

- **Song Chart Words** Display the words *trail*, *rain*, and *stain* from the Word Wall Starters pack. Ask if anyone recognizes the words. Compare the words to *trail*, *rain*, and *stain* on the chart page. Invite children to tell you what letters are highlighted in yellow on each card. Place the cards *trail*, *rain*, and *stain* beneath the *long a* label, taking care to group word families together. Later as children encounter additional long *a* words in their reading and other class work, write each new word on an index card and highlight the long *a* phonogram. Add these words to this section of your Word Wall as well.
- **Big Book Word** After you have read the Big Book *What Fine Gardeners*, display the word *pail* from the Word Wall Starters pack. Using the word card and the Big Book, use a routine similar to the one above, and place the word card *pail* beneath the other *ail* word family words.

Assessment for STAGES

❶❷ Although these children may participate in word family instruction, they should not be expected to master or apply it.

❸ Say the word *Gail* and have the child point to the word on the chart page. Identify the letters *ail* together and underline them with your finger. Invite him or her to identify which of the following words also belongs to the *ail* word family: *letter, mail, stamp*. As desired, use a similar routine for the *ain* word family.

❹❺ Say the word *Gail* and have the child point to the word on the chart page. Ask him or her to identify the letters *ail* and underline them with a finger. Have the child think of another word that has the *ail* sound as in *Gail* in it. If he or she needs help, sing the song together and encourage the child to identify a word in the song. As desired, use a similar routine for the *ain* word family.

Take-Home Phonics Story

Reading the Book in Class

- Distribute copies of pages 39–40 from the Take-Home Phonics Stories. Have children create their own books.
- For Emergent readers, read one of the books created by a child to a small group of four to six children one or more times. For Early readers, you can skip this step.
- Invite children to buddy read the book in pairs of heterogeneous stages.
- As they seem ready, have children read the book independently.

Word Bank

ail		ain	
bail	pail	main	plain
fail	rail	pain	slain
Gail	sail	rain	Spain
hail	tail	brain	sprain
jail	wail	chain	stain
mail	snail	drain	strain
nail	trail	grain	train

Connecting to Home

- Tell children to take the books they made home to share with their families once they are able to read them independently.
- Be sure to include the Parent Letter from pages 3–10 of the Take-Home Phonics Stories in the appropriate home language when you send home the book made by each child.

Phonics Song Chart 15   The *ail* and *ain* Word Families

The *oke* and *ope* Word Families

Setting the Scene

- Have children pretend that it is Saturday morning. Tell them to imagine that they have just awakened, looked outside, and discovered that it is raining. Ask children if this ever happened to them before. Allow them to share their experiences.
- Then ask them to think about one outdoor activity they wish they could be doing. Invite a volunteer to act out the activity and have children guess what it is.

Creating Comprehensible Input

- Say the chant slowly as you use gestures and pointing to make it comprehensible.

When I woke up, I started to hope	point to yourself, rub your eyes, then point to yourself
That if it stopped raining, I could jump rope.	point to the rain, point to yourself, then point to the jump rope
Mom told a joke that got me to smile.	point to the mother, then smile and point to your lips
I hope I can jump rope in a short while.	point to yourself and to the jump rope, then point to your watch

Singing and Gestures

- Sing the song together as you play it on the Phonics Audio CD. Once they learn the song, teach children gestures they can make as they sing it again.
- As they begin to sing, have them pretend they are waking up.
- Each time they sing *jump rope*, ask children to pretend they are jumping rope.

Recognizing the *oke* and *ope* Word Families

- Sing the first line of the song, then point to the word *woke* as you say it. Write it on the board or easel pad and say the word again. Point to the letters *oke* and tell children that the letters *oke* stand for the last two sounds they hear in *woke*, even though there are three letters. Ask if they can find another word that sounds like *woke*. [joke] Write the word *joke* under the word *woke*. Ask volunteers for any other words they can think of that rhyme with *woke*. Bear in mind that only children in Stages 3–5 will be able to brainstorm English words based on sounds.
- Invite children to pretend they just woke up by stretching each time they hear the *oke* sound as in *woke* as you say the following words: *broke, fix, smoke, hot, rain, poke, like, jump, spoke, talk*.
- Continue this procedure for words that rhyme with *hope*.

Exploring Sound-Symbol Relationships

- Use a small sticky note to cover up the first letter of each word on the chart page that ends with *oke* or *ope*. This will encourage children to focus on the print of *oke* and *ope*.
- After removing the sticky notes, invite children to come up to the chart page and practice underlining the letters that make the *oke* sound as in *woke* and the *ope* sound as in *hope* with their fingers.

CHART 16

When I woke up,
I started to hope
That if it stopped raining,
I could jump rope.
Mom told a joke
that got me to smile.
I hope I can jump rope
in a short while.

Sung to the tune of "Rockabye, Baby"

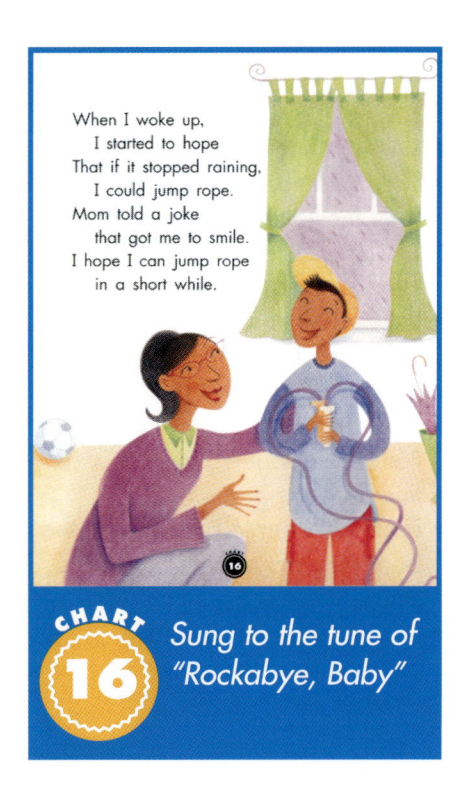

Extending to the *ose* Word Family

Sung to the tune of "Rockabye, Baby"

I go outside by my garden hose.
I see some daisies and a pink rose.
I do suppose I'll pick this pink rose.
Then I will smell the rose that I chose!

Language Junction

The Hmong language does not have a long *o* sound, so children whose home language is Hmong might have difficulty producing the sound at first. Their pronunciation will gradually improve over time.

STAGES: ① Preproduction ② Early Production ③ Speech Emergence ④ Intermediate Fluency ⑤ Advanced Fluency

Writing Words from the *oke* and *ope* Word Families

- Encourage children to use their phonics skills in writing. Put away the chart page and write the following sentence on the board or easel pad:
  When I _____ up, I started to _____.
- Ask volunteers to tell you what goes in the first blank. Invite the group to say the word *woke* together, stretching the sounds.
- Ask children to tell you what letter to start *woke* with as you write it down on the board or easel pad. Invite volunteers to come up and write the remaining letters using their phonics skills to match sounds and letters.
- Have children use their own paper to practice writing the letters in the word *woke*.
- Use a similar procedure for the word *hope* in the second blank in the sentence.
- When you are finished, display the chart page and invite children to make comparisons between the words *woke* and *hope* on the chart page and the same words on their own papers. Going back to the original print encourages children to use print resources in their spelling.

Using Word Wall Starters

- **Song Chart Words** Display the words *joke*, *hope*, and *rope* from the Word Wall Starters pack. Ask if anyone recognizes the words. Compare the words to *joke*, *hope*, and *rope* on the chart page. Invite children to tell you what letters are highlighted in yellow on each card. Use the *long o* label to start the long o section of your Word Wall and place the cards *joke*, *hope*, and *rope* beneath it. Be sure to group word families together. Later as children encounter additional long o words in their reading and other class work, write each new word on an index card and highlight the long o phonogram. Add these words to the appropriate section of your Word Wall as well.
- **Big Book Word** After you have read the Big Book *What Fine Gardeners*, display the word *woke* from the Word Wall Starters pack. Using the word card and the Big Book, use a routine similar to the one above, and place the word card *woke* beneath the other *oke* word family words.

Assessment for STAGES

❶❷ Although these children may participate in word family instruction, they should not be expected to master or apply it.

❸ Say the word *woke* and have the child point to the word on the chart page. Identify the letters *oke* together and underline them with your finger. Invite him or her to identify which of the following words also belongs to the *oke* word family: *talk*, *speak*, *spoke*. As desired, use a similar routine for the *ope* word family.

❹❺ Say the word *woke* and have the child point to the word on the chart page. Ask him or her to identify the letters *oke* and underline them with a finger. Have the child think of another word that has the sound *oke* as in *woke* in it. If he or she needs help, sing the song together and encourage the child to identify a word in the song. As desired, use a similar routine for the *ope* word family.

Take-Home Phonics Story

Reading the Book in Class
- Distribute copies of pages 41–42 from the Take-Home Phonics Stories. Have children create their own books.
- For Emergent readers, read one of the books created by a child to a small group of four to six children one or more times. For Early readers, you can skip this step.
- Invite children to buddy read the book in pairs of heterogeneous stages.
- As they seem ready, have children read the book independently.

Word Bank

oke		ope	
joke	choke	cope	rope
poke	smoke	hope	grope
woke	spoke	mope	scope
yoke	stoke	pope	slope
broke	stroke		

Connecting to Home

- Tell children to take the books they made home to share with their families once they are able to read them independently.
- Be sure to include the Parent Letter from pages 3–10 of the Take-Home Phonics Stories in the appropriate home language when you send home the book made by each child.

The *oad* and *old* Word Families

Setting the Scene

- Obtain a book about toads from the library. As you show the pictures in the book to the class, explain that toads are like frogs. Show a close-up picture of a toad and point out the toad's rough, dry, brown skin.
- Invite children to pretend they are toads or frogs, encouraging them to squat low and leap around the room.

Creating Comprehensible Input

- Say the chant slowly as you use gestures and pointing to make it comprehensible.

Old Mister Toad told the young toad,	point to the old toad, then point to the young toad
"I have a very bad cold."	point to yourself, then pretend to blow your nose
Old Mister Toad told the young toad,	point to the old toad, then point to the young toad
"Please make some soup for my cold!"	point to the pot of soup, then pretend to blow your nose

Singing and Gestures

- Sing the song together as you play it on the Phonics Audio CD. Once they learn the song, teach children gestures they can make as they sing it again.
- Divide the class into pairs. As they sing, have one child pretend to be Old Mister Toad, while the other child pretends to be the young toad. Have the child playing the young toad sing the first and third lines while pretending to prepare soup. Have the child playing Old Mister Toad sing the second and fourth lines while holding a hand to his or her forehead.

Recognizing the *oad* and *old* Word Families

- Sing the first line of the song, then point to the word *Old* as you say it. Write it on the board or easel pad and say the word again. Ask if they can find any words that sound like *Old*. [*told, cold*] Write these words under the word *Old*. Ask volunteers for any other words they can think of that rhyme with *Old*. Bear in mind that only children in Stages 3–5 will be able to brainstorm English words based on sounds.
- Invite children to pretend they are blowing their noses each time they hear a word that sounds like *Old* as you say the following: *bold, laugh, mold, grass, rose, hold, note, fold, gold, red*.
- Continue in a similar manner for words that rhyme with *Toad*.

Exploring Sound-Symbol Relationships

- Use a small sticky note to cover up the first letter of each word on the chart page that ends with *oad* or *old*. This will encourage children to focus on the print of *oad* and *old*.
- After removing the sticky notes, invite children to come up to the chart page and practice underlining the letters that make the *oad* sound as in *toad* and the *old* sound as in *told* with their fingers.

CHART 17
Sung to the tune of "My Bonnie Lies Over the Ocean"

Old Mister Toad told the young toad,
"I have a very bad cold."
Old Mister Toad told the young toad,
"Please make some soup for my cold!"

Extending to the *ow* Word Families

Sung to the tune of "My Bonnie Lies Over the Ocean"

I'm hearing the cold winter wind blow.
I know it will soon start to snow.
Look out the window. I'll show you.
I think you'll agree it will snow!

Language Junction

The range of final consonant blends is much smaller in Arabic, and none of those in Arabic exist in English. As a result, children whose native language is Arabic may have difficulties with final consonant blends. Arabic speakers tend to insert vowels between the sounds in consonant blends, such as /ld/, to make them easier to pronounce.

STAGES ① Preproduction ② Early Production ③ Speech Emergence ④ Intermediate Fluency ⑤ Advanced Fluency

Writing Words from the *oad* and *old* Word Families

- Encourage children to use their phonics skills in writing. Put away the chart page and write the following sentence on the board or easel pad:
  Old Mister Toad _____ the young _____, "I have a very bad cold."
- Ask volunteers to tell you what goes in the first blank. Invite the group to say the word *told* together, stretching the sounds.
- Ask children to tell you what letter to start *told* with as you write it down on the board or easel pad. Invite volunteers to come up and write the remaining letters using their phonics skills to match sounds and letters.
- Have children use their own paper to practice writing the letters in the word *told*.
- Use a similar procedure for the word *toad* in the second blank in the sentence.
- When you are finished, display the chart page and invite children to make comparisons between the words *told* and *toad* on the chart page and the same words on their own papers. Going back to the original print encourages children to use print resources in their spelling.

Using Word Wall Starters

- **Song Chart Words** Display the words *toad*, *old*, and *cold* from the Word Wall Starters pack. Ask if anyone recognizes the words. Compare the words to *Toad*, *Old*, and *cold* on the chart page. Invite children to tell you what letters are highlighted in yellow on each card. Place the cards *toad*, *old*, and *cold* beneath the *long o* label, taking care to group word families together. Later as children encounter additional long *o* words in their reading and other class work, write each new word on an index card and highlight the long *o* phonogram. Add these words to this section of your Word Wall as well.
- **Big Book Word** After you have read the Big Book *What Fine Gardeners*, display the word *road* from the Word Wall Starters pack. Using the word card and the Big Book, use a routine similar to the one above, and place the card *road* beneath the other *oad* word family words.

Assessment for STAGES

❶❷ Although these children may participate in word family instruction, they should not be expected to master or apply it.

❸ Say the word *told* and have the child point to the word on the chart page. Identify the letters *old* together and underline them with your finger. Invite him or her to identify which of the following words also belongs to the *old* word family: *iron*, *wash*, *fold*. As desired, use a similar routine for the *oad* word family.

❹❺ Say the word *told* and have the child point to the word on the chart page. Ask him or her to identify the letters *old* and underline them with a finger. Have the child think of another word that has the sound *old* as in *told* in it. If he or she needs assistance, sing the song together and encourage the child to identify a word in the song. As desired, use a similar routine for the *oad* word family.

Take-Home Phonics Story

Reading the Book in Class
- Distribute copies of pages 43–44 from the Take-Home Phonics Stories. Have children create their own books.
- For Emergent readers, read one of the books created by a child to a small group of four to six children one or more times. For Early readers, you can skip this step.
- Invite children to buddy read the book in pairs of heterogeneous stages.
- As they seem ready, have children read the book independently.

Word Bank

oad	old	
load	bold	mold
road	cold	old
toad	fold	sold
	gold	told
	hold	scold

Connecting to Home

- Tell children to take the books they made home to share with their families once they are able to read them independently.
- Be sure to include the Parent Letter from pages 3–10 of the Take-Home Phonics Stories in the appropriate home language when you send home the book made by each child.

Phonics Song Chart 17   *The oad and old Word Families*

*I like to ride
  my bike all day long.
I like to ride
  while I sing a song.
When I see Mike,
  we ride side by side.
We ride to the park
  then go down the slide.*

CHART 18 *Sung to the tune of "Rockabye, Baby"*

Extending to the *ine* Word Families

*Sung to the tune of "Rockabye, Baby"
This week I turn nine.
My mom will bake.
We will all dine
  on my birthday cake.
My birthday cake
  will taste oh so fine.
We'll celebrate
  in rain or sunshine!*

Language Junction

Children who are familiar with the written form of the following languages may have transfer difficulty decoding the letter *i*: Spanish, Hmong, Vietnamese, and Haitian Creole. These children may tend to produce the long *e* for the letter *i*. In addition, these children may need to be reminded not to pronounce the final *e* in words whose written forms end in *ike* or *ide*. Expect negative transfer to lessen as learners gain familiarity with English print.

P40

The *ike* and *ide* Word Families

Setting the Scene
- Ask children if they have a bike or have ever ridden a bike. Encourage them to talk about what their bikes look like, where they ride, and so on.

Creating Comprehensible Input
- Say the chant slowly as you use gestures and pointing to make it comprehensible.

I like to ride my bike all day long.	point to yourself, pretend you are holding bicycle handlebars, then point to one of the bikes
I like to ride while I sing a song.	point to yourself, pretend you are holding handlebars, point to yourself, then cup hands around your mouth
When I see Mike, we ride side by side.	point to yourself, point to one of the boys, then point to both boys and their bikes
We ride to the park then go down the slide.	pretend you are holding bicycle handlebars, point to the park, then point to the slide

Singing and Gestures
- Sing the song together as you play it on the Phonics Audio CD. Once they learn the song, teach children gestures they can make as they sing the song.
- Ask children to sit in their chairs. Each time they sing the word *I*, have them point to themselves. When they sing the word *ride*, have them pretend they are holding their handlebars as they move their feet on the pedals.

Recognizing the *ike* and *ide* Word Families
- Sing the first line of the song, then point to the word *like* as you say it. Write it on the board or easel pad and say the word again. Point to the letters *ike* and tell children that the letters *ike* stand for the last two sounds they hear in *like*, even though there are three letters. Ask if they can find any other words that sound similar to *like*. [bike, Mike] Write these words under the word *like*. Ask volunteers for any other words they can think of that rhyme with *like*. Bear in mind that only children in Stages 3–5 will be able to brainstorm English words based on sounds.
- Invite children to pretend they are holding their handlebars each time they hear the *ike* sound as in *like* as you say the following words: *bike, walk, jump, Mark, Jan, strike, run, spike, tree, pine*.
- Continue this routine for words that rhyme with *ride*.

Exploring Sound-Symbol Relationships
- Use a small sticky note to cover up the first letter or letters of each word on the chart page that ends with *ike* or *ide*. This will encourage children to focus on the print of *ike* and *ide*.
- After removing the sticky notes, invite children to come up to the chart page and practice underlining the letters that make the *ike* sound as in *like* and the *ide* sound as in *ride* with their fingers.

STAGES ① Preproduction ② Early Production ③ Speech Emergence ④ Intermediate Fluency ⑤ Advanced Fluency

Writing Words from the *ike* and *ide* Word Families

- Encourage children to use their phonics skills in writing. Put away the chart page and write the following sentence on the board or easel pad:
    When I see _____, we _____ side by side.
- Ask volunteers to tell you what goes in the first blank. Invite the group to say the word *Mike* together, stretching the sounds.
- Ask children to tell you what letter to start *Mike* with as you write it down on the board or easel pad. Invite volunteers to come up and write the remaining letters using their phonics skills to match sounds and letters.
- Have children use their own paper to practice writing the letters in the word *Mike*.
- Use a similar procedure for the word *ride* in the second blank in the sentence.
- When you are finished, display the chart page and invite children to make comparisons between the words *Mike* and *ride* on the chart page and the same words on their own papers. Going back to the original print encourages children to use print resources in their spelling.

Using Word Wall Starters

- **Song Chart Words** Display the words *bike, ride,* and *side* from the Word Wall Starters pack. Ask if anyone recognizes the words. Compare the words to *bike, ride,* and *side* on the chart page. Invite children to tell you what letters are highlighted in yellow on each card. Use the *long i* label to start the long *i* section of your Word Wall and place the cards *bike, ride,* and *side* beneath it. Be sure to group word families together. Later as children encounter additional long *i* words in their reading and other class work, write each new word on an index card and highlight the long *i* phonogram. Add these words to this section of your Word Wall as well.
- **Big Book Word** After you have read the Big Book *Water Detective*, display the word *like* from the Word Wall Starters pack. Using the word card and the Big Book, use a routine similar to the one above, and place the word card *like* beneath the other *ike* word family words.

Assessment for STAGES

❶❷ Although these children may participate in word family instruction, they should not be expected to master or apply it.

❸ Say the word *like* and have the child point to the word on the chart page. Identify the letters *ike* together and underline them with your finger. Invite him or her to identify which of the following words also belongs to the *ike* word family: *hop, hike, run*. As desired, use a similar routine for the *ide* word family.

❹❺ Say the word *like* and have the child point to the word on the chart page. Ask him or her to identify the letters *ike* and underline them with a finger. Have the child think of another word that has the sound *ike* as in *like* in it. If he or she needs help, sing the song together and encourage the child to identify a word in the song. As desired, use a similar routine for the *ide* word family.

Take-Home Phonics Story

Reading the Book in Class
- Distribute copies of pages 45–46 from the Take-Home Phonics Stories. Have children create their own books.
- For Emergent readers, read one of the books created by a child to a small group of four to six children one or more times. For Early readers, you can skip this step.
- Invite children to buddy read the book in pairs of heterogeneous stages.
- As they seem ready, have children read the book independently.

Word Bank

ike		ide	
bike	Mike	hide	wide
hike	spike	ride	bride
like	strike	side	pride
		tide	slide

Connecting to Home

- Tell children to take the books they made home to share with their families once they are able to read them independently.
- Be sure to include the Parent Letter from pages 3–10 of the Take-Home Phonics Stories in the appropriate home language when you send home the book made by each child.

Phonics Song Chart 18   The *ike* and *ide* Word Families

I'll make a pie just right.
It will be quite a sight.
I'll eat my pie and then lie down
Because my pants are tight!

CHART 19
Sung to the tune of "The Farmer in the Dell"

The *ie* and *ight* Word Families

Setting the Scene

- Bring in pictures of different kinds of pie and say *pie*, inviting children to repeat the word after you. Explain that there are many kinds of pies, including fruit pies. Ask children to think of fruits that are put into pies, such as apples, blueberries, and peaches. Ask children if they have ever eaten pie. Finally take a vote to see what kind of pie is the classroom favorite!
- Bring in some prepared pie dough and rolling pins. Invite each child to roll some dough into a ball and then flatten it out with a rolling pin.

Creating Comprehensible Input

- Say the chant slowly as you use gestures and pointing to make it comprehensible.

I'll make a pie just right.	point to yourself, then to the pie
It will be quite a sight.	hold your hands out and smile
I'll eat my pie and then lie down	point to yourself, pretend to eat a piece of pie, then pretend to lie down
Because my pants are tight!	point to yourself, then to your stomach

Singing and Gestures

- Sing the song together as you play it on the Phonics Audio CD. Once they learn the song, teach children gestures they can make as they sing it again.
- As children sing the first two lines, have them pretend to roll out pie dough.
- On the last two lines of the song, have children pretend to eat their pie, and then to lie down and hold their stomachs.

Recognizing the *ie* and *ight* Word Families

- Sing the first line of the song, then point to the word *pie* as you say it. Write it on the board or easel pad and say the word again. Point to the letters *ie* and tell children that the letters *ie* stand for the last sound they hear in *pie*, even though there are two letters. Ask if they can find another word that sounds like *pie*. [*lie*] Write the word *lie* under the word *pie*. Ask volunteers for any other words they can think of that rhyme with *pie*. Bear in mind that only children in Stages 3–5 will be able to brainstorm English words based on sounds.
- Invite children to pretend they are eating a piece of pie each time they hear the *ie* sound as in *pie* as you say the following words: *bow, ring, tie, sock, lie, cake, die, win, cone, hat*.
- Use a similar routine for words that rhyme with *right*.

Exploring Sound-Symbol Relationships

- Use a small sticky note to cover up the first letter of each word on the chart page that ends with *ie* or *ight*. This will encourage children to focus on the print of *ie* and *ight*.
- After removing the sticky notes, invite children to come up to the chart page and practice underlining the letters that make the *ie* sound as in *pie* and the *ight* sound as in *right* with their fingers.

Language Junction

The letters *gh* in Spanish never form part of the spelling of a vowel sound as they do in English. Children familiar with Spanish print need to learn that the letters are silent in English.

STAGES ① Preproduction ② Early Production ③ Speech Emergence ④ Intermediate Fluency ⑤ Advanced Fluency

Writing Words from the *ie* and *ight* Word Families

- Encourage children to use their phonics skills in writing. Put away the chart page and write the following sentence on the board or easel pad:

    I'll make a _____ just _____.

- Ask volunteers to tell you what goes in the first blank. Invite the group to say the word *pie* together, stretching the sounds.
- Ask children to tell you what letter to start *pie* with as you write it down on the board or easel pad. Invite volunteers to come up and write the remaining letters using their phonics skills to match sounds and letters.
- Have children use their own paper to practice writing the letters in the word *pie*.
- Use a similar procedure for the word *right* in the second blank in the sentence.
- When you are finished, display the chart page and invite children to make comparisons between the words *pie* and *right* on the chart page and the same words on their own papers. Going back to the original print encourages children to use print resources in their spelling.

Using Word Wall Starters

- **Song Chart Words** Display the words *pie, lie,* and *sight* from the Word Wall Starters pack. Ask if anyone recognizes the words. Compare the words to *pie, lie,* and *sight* on the chart page. Invite children to tell you what letters are highlighted in yellow on each card. Place the cards *pie, lie,* and *sight* beneath the *long i* label, taking care to group word families together. Later as children encounter additional long *i* words in their reading and other class work, write each new word on an index card and highlight the long *i* phonogram. Add these words to this section of your Word Wall as well.
- **Big Book Word** After you have read the Big Book *Water Detective*, display the word *right* from the Word Wall Starters pack. Using the word card and the Big Book, use a routine similar to the one above, and place the word card *right* beneath the other *ight* word family words.

Assessment for STAGES

❶❷ Although these children may participate in word family instruction, they should not be expected to master or apply it.

❸ Say the word *pie* and have the child point to the word on the chart page. Identify the letters *ie* together and underline them with your finger. Invite him or her to identify which of the following words also belongs to the *ie* word family: *bow, shirt, tie.* As desired, use a similar routine for the *ight* word family.

❹❺ Say the word *pie* and have the child point to the word on the chart page. Ask him or her to identify the letters *ie* and underline them with a finger. Have the child think of another word that has the *ie* sound as in *pie* in it. If he or she needs assistance, sing the song together and encourage the child to identify a word in the song. As desired, use a similar routine for the *ight* word family.

Take-Home Phonics Story

Reading the Book in Class
- Distribute copies of pages 47–48 from the Take-Home Phonics Stories. Have children create their own books.
- For Emergent readers, read one of the books created by a child to a small group of four to six children one or more times. For Early readers, you can skip this step.
- Invite children to buddy read the book in pairs of heterogeneous stages.
- As they seem ready, have children read the book independently.

Word Bank

ie	ight	
die	light	sight
lie	might	tight
pie	night	bright
tie	right	flight

Connecting to Home

- Tell children to take the books they made home to share with their families once they are able to read them independently.
- Be sure to include the Parent Letter from pages 3–10 of the Take-Home Phonics Stories in the appropriate home language when you send home the book made by each child.

CHART 21 — *Sung to the tune of "Skip to My Lou"*

Let's pretend that we can fly.
Let's pretend we're in the sky.
Fly with me. Please won't you try?
Let's be birds up in the sky!

Words with -y

Setting the Scene
- Pretend you are a bird flying in the air. Then ask children to guess what animal you are pretending to be. Once children have guessed, invite them to pretend they are high-flying birds!

Creating Comprehensible Input
- Say the chant slowly as you use gestures and pointing to make it comprehensible.

Let's pretend that we can fly.	point to the class, then hold your arms out as if you are flying
Let's pretend we're in the sky.	point to the class, then point up to the sky
Fly with me. Please won't you try?	hold your arms out as if you are flying
Let's be birds up in the sky!	point to the class, then to the birds

Singing and Gestures
- Sing the song together as you play it on the Phonics Audio CD. Once they learn the song, teach children gestures they can make as they sing it again.
- Each time children sing the word *fly*, have them pretend they are birds flying above treetops and houses.
- Each time they sing *sky*, have them point upwards.

Recognizing Words with -y
- Sing the first line of the song, then point to the word *fly* as you say it. Write it on the board or easel pad and say the word again. Point to the letter *y* and tell children that the letter *y* stands for the last sound they hear in *fly*. Ask if they can find any other words that sound like *fly*. [*sky, try*] Write these words under the word *fly*. Tell children that there are many other words that end in *y* as *fly* does. Ask volunteers for any other words they can think of that rhyme with *fly*. Bear in mind that only children in Stages 3–5 will be able to brainstorm English words based on sounds.
- Invite children to pretend they are flying each time they hear *y* as in *fly* as you say the following words: *by, bee, my, his, cry, spy, saw, dry, why, has*.

Exploring Sound-Symbol Relationships
- Use a small sticky note to cover up the first two letters of each word on the chart page that ends with *y* as in *fly*. This will encourage children to focus on the print of *y*.
- After removing the sticky notes, invite children to come up to the chart page and practice underlining the letter that makes *y* as in *fly* with their fingers.

Language Junction
Children from most language backgrounds should have success in producing the sound of long *i* that the letter *y* stands for at the end of words such as *cry*. However, in decoding, children may initially overgeneralize and read English words like *many* with the long *i* sound at the end.

P46

STAGES ① Preproduction ② Early Production ③ Speech Emergence ④ Intermediate Fluency ⑤ Advanced Fluency

Writing Words with -y

- Encourage children to use their phonics skills in writing. Put away the chart page and write the following sentences on the board or easel pad:

  _____ *with me. Please won't you* _____?

- Ask volunteers to tell you what goes in the first blank. Invite the group to say *Fly* together, stretching the sounds.
- Ask children to tell you what letter to start *Fly* with as you write it down on the board or easel pad. Invite volunteers to come up and write the remaining letters using their phonics skills to match sounds and letters.
- Have children use their own paper to practice writing the letters in the word *Fly*.
- Use a similar procedure for the word *try* in the blank in the next sentence.
- When you are finished, display the chart page and invite children to make comparisons between the words *Fly* and *try* on the chart page and the same words on their own papers. Going back to the original print encourages children to use print resources in their spelling.

Using Word Wall Starters

- **Song Chart Words** Display the word *fly* from the Word Wall Starters pack. Ask if anyone recognizes the word. Compare the word to *fly* on the chart page. Invite children to tell you what letter is highlighted in yellow on the card. Use the -y label to start this section of your Word Wall and place the card *fly* beneath it. Later as children encounter additional words that end with *y* as in *fly* in their reading and other class work, write each new word on an index card and highlight the ending *y*. Add these words to this section of your Word Wall as well.
- **Big Book Word** After you have read the Big Book *Water Detective*, display the word *my* from the Word Wall Starters pack. Using the word card and the Big Book, use a routine similar to the one above, and place the card *my* beneath the other words that end with *y* as in *fly*.

Assessment for STAGES

❶❷ Although these children may participate in this instruction, they should not be expected to master or apply it.

❸ Say the word *fly* and have the child point to the word on the chart page. Identify the letter *y* together and underline it with your finger. Invite him or her to identify which of the following words also end with *y* as in *fly*: *near, on, by*.

❹❺ Say the word *fly* and have the child point to the word on the chart page. Ask him or her to identify the letter *y* and underline it with a finger. Have the child think of another word that ends with *y* as in *fly*. If he or she needs assistance, sing the song together and encourage the child to identify a word in the song.

Take-Home Phonics Story

Reading the Book in Class
- Distribute copies of pages 51–52 from the Take-Home Phonics Stories. Have children create their own books.
- For Emergent readers, read one of the books created by a child to a small group of four to six children one or more times. For Early readers, you can skip this step.
- Invite children to buddy read the book in pairs of heterogeneous stages.
- As they seem ready, have children read the book independently.

Word Bank

-y (as in *fly*)

cry	July
dry	my
fly	try
fry	why

Connecting to Home

- Tell children to take the books they made home to share with their families once they are able to read them independently.
- Be sure to include the Parent Letter from pages 3–10 of the Take-Home Phonics Stories in the appropriate home language when you send home the book made by each child.

Words with Long u (uCe)

Setting the Scene

- Tell children that they're going to have a party, starting right now! Mention that it's going to be a party where they will sing lots of tunes. Say the word *tunes*, and invite children to echo you. Explain that *tunes* is another word for *songs*. Have children brainstorm their favorite tunes to sing, and write each title on the board. Then have a "tuneful" celebration!

Creating Comprehensible Input

- Say the chant slowly as you use gestures and pointing to make it comprehensible.

When June has a party, we're sure to have fun.	point to the girl carrying two balloons, then point to the class and smile
We'll play flute and sing tunes.	point to the flute, then to the boy who is singing
We'll skip and we'll run.	point to the children skipping and running

Singing and Gestures

- Sing the song together as you play it on the Phonics Audio CD. Once they learn the song, teach children gestures they can make as they sing it again.
- As children sing the first two lines of the song, have them act out holding balloons.
- On the third line, have children pretend they are playing flutes.
- On the last line, ask them to skip or run in place as they sing.

Recognizing Long u (uCe) Words

- Sing the first line of the song, then point to the word *June* as you say it. Write it on the board or easel pad and say the word again. Point to the letters *une* and tell children that the letters *une* stand for the last two sounds they hear in *June*, even though there are three letters. Ask if they can find another word that sounds almost like *June*. [*tunes*] Write the word *tunes* under the word *June*. Ask volunteers for any other words they can think of that end in the *une* sound as in *June*. Bear in mind that only children in Stages 3–5 will be able to brainstorm English words based on sounds.
- Invite children to pretend they are singing a tune each time they hear the *une* sound as in *June* as you say the following words: *bake, time, clip, prune, dig, dune, pack, box, tune, ear*.
- Continue this routine for words that rhyme with *flute*. Tell children that both *June* and *flute* have the long *u* sound.

Exploring Sound-Symbol Relationships

- Use a small sticky note to cover up the first letter or letters of each word on the chart page that ends with *une* or *ute*. This will encourage children to focus on the print of *une* and *ute*.
- After removing the sticky notes, invite children to come up to the chart page and practice underlining the letters that make the *une* sound in *June* and the *ute* sound in *flute* with their fingers.

CHART 22 — Sung to the tune of "On Top of Old Smokey"

When June has a party, we're sure to have fun. We'll play flute and sing tunes. We'll skip and we'll run.

Language Junction

English vowels differ in length—such as the long *u* as in *rule* versus the vowel sound in *book*. Children whose native language does not have vowels that differ in length in this way may need some help with the sound of long *u* as in *rule*. This challenge may affect speakers of Spanish, Vietnamese, Cantonese, and Korean. Speakers of these languages may produce a sound that is between the two English vowels.

STAGES ① Preproduction ② Early Production ③ Speech Emergence ④ Intermediate Fluency ⑤ Advanced Fluency

Writing Words with Long *u* (uCe)

- Encourage children to use their phonics skills in writing. Put away the chart page and write the following sentences on the board or easel pad:
   When _____ has a party, we're sure to have fun.
   We'll play _____ and sing tunes.
- Ask volunteers to tell you what goes in the first blank. Invite the group to say *June* together, stretching the sounds.
- Ask children to tell you what letter to start *June* with as you write it down on the board or easel pad. Invite volunteers to come up and write the remaining letters using their phonics skills to match sounds and letters.
- Have children use their own paper to practice writing the letters in the word *June*.
- Use a similar procedure for the word *flute* in the second sentence.
- When you are finished, display the chart page and invite children to make comparisons between the words *June* and *flute* on the chart page and the same words on their own papers. Going back to the original print encourages children to use print resources in their spelling.

Using Word Wall Starters

- **Song Chart Word** Display the word *June* from the Word Wall Starters pack. Ask if anyone recognizes the word. Compare the word to *June* on the chart page. Invite children to tell you what letters are highlighted in yellow on the card. Use the *long u* label to start the long *u* section of your Word Wall and place the card *June* beneath it. Later as children encounter additional long *u* words in their reading and other class work, write each new word on an index card and highlight the long *u* phonogram. Add these words to this section of your Word Wall as well, taking care to group word families together.
- **Big Book Word** After you have read the Big Book *Barge Cat*, display the word *huge* from the Word Wall Starters pack. Using the word card and the Big Book, use a routine similar to the one above, and place the card *huge* beneath the other long *u* words.

Assessment for STAGES

❶❷ Although these children may participate in long *u* instruction, they should not be expected to master or apply it.

❸ Say the word *June* and have the child point to the word on the chart page. Identify the letters *une* together and underline them with your finger. Invite him or her to identify which of the following words also belongs to the *une* word family: *lake, dune, desert*. As desired, use a similar routine for the *ute* word family.

❹❺ Say the word *June* and have the child point to the word on the chart page. Ask him or her to identify the letters *une* and underline them with a finger. Have the child think of another word that has the sound *une* as in *June* in it. If he or she needs assistance, sing the song together and encourage the child to identify a word in the song. As desired, use a similar routine for the *ute* word family.

Take-Home Phonics Story

Reading the Book in Class

- Distribute copies of pages 53–54 from the Take-Home Phonics Stories. Have children create their own books.
- For Emergent readers, read one of the books created by a child to a small group of four to six children one or more times. For Early readers, you can skip this step.
- Invite children to buddy read the book in pairs of heterogeneous stages.
- As they seem ready, have children read the book independently.

Word Bank

Long u (uCe)

cube	Lupe
cute	lute
dude	mule
duke	mute
dune	prune
flute	rude
fuse	rule
June	tube
Luke	tune

Connecting to Home

- Tell children to take the books they made home to share with their families once they are able to read them independently.
- Be sure to include the Parent Letter from pages 3–10 of the Take-Home Phonics Stories in the appropriate home language when you send home the book made by each child.

Phonics Song Chart 22   Words with Long u (uCe)   **P49**

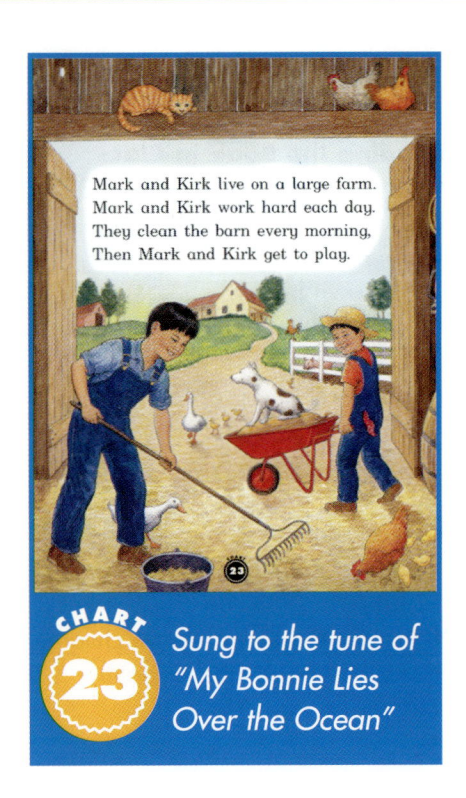

Mark and Kirk live on a large farm.
Mark and Kirk work hard each day.
They clean the barn every morning,
Then Mark and Kirk get to play.

CHART 23 Sung to the tune of "My Bonnie Lies Over the Ocean"

Language Junction

The vowels that occur before *r* in English are pronounced somewhat differently from vowels that occur in other places. As a result, learners from many language backgrounds may have difficulty pronouncing *r*-controlled vowels. Accept approximations at first.

P50

Words with *R*-Controlled Vowels

Setting the Scene

- Ask children if they have ever been on a farm. Encourage them to share their experiences with the class.
- Invite volunteers to pretend they are working on a farm. Have them pretend to do farm chores, such as raking the barn floor, or feeding the chickens.

Creating Comprehensible Input

- Say the chant slowly as you use gestures and pointing to make it comprehensible.

Mark and Kirk live on a large farm.	point to both boys, then point to the farm
Mark and Kirk work hard each day.	wipe your forehead
They clean the barn every morning.	point to the rake and the wheelbarrow
Then Mark and Kirk get to play.	run in place

Singing and Gestures

- Sing the song together as you play it on the Phonics Audio CD.
- Have them open their arms wide as they sing the word *large* in the first line.
- On the second line, have children wipe their foreheads.
- On the third line, have children act out raking the floor of a barn.
- As they sing the last line, have children act out running off to play.

Recognizing *R*-Controlled Vowels

- Sing the first line of the song, then point to the word *Mark* as you say it. Write it on the board or easel pad and say the word again. Point to the letters *ar* and tell children that the letters *ar* stand for the middle sound they hear in *Mark*. Ask if they can find any other words that have the *ar* sound as in *Mark*. [large, farm, hard, barn] Write these words under the word *Mark*. Ask volunteers for any other words they can think of that have this sound. Bear in mind that only children in Stages 3–5 will be able to brainstorm English words based on sounds.
- Invite children to pretend they are raking the floor of a barn each time they hear the *ar* sound as in *Mark* as you say the following words: *cart, wagon, arm, handle, giggle, charm, letter, card, star, circle*.
- Continue this routine for words that have *ir, er,* and *or*.

Exploring Sound-Symbol Relationships

- Locate all of the words on the chart page that include *ar*. Then use a small sticky note with arrows drawn on it to point to the *ar* in each of these words. This will encourage children to focus on the print of *ar*.
- After removing the sticky notes, invite children to come up to the chart page and practice underlining the letters that make the *ar* sound as in *Mark* in each word with their fingers. Then continue this routine for words that have *ir, er,* and *or*.

STAGES ❶ Preproduction ❷ Early Production ❸ Speech Emergence ❹ Intermediate Fluency ❺ Advanced Fluency

Writing Words with *R*-Controlled Vowels

- Encourage children to use their phonics skills in writing. Put away the chart page and write the following sentence on the board or easel pad:
  _____ and _____ work hard each day.
- Ask volunteers to tell you what goes in the first blank. Invite the group to say the word *Mark* together, stretching the sounds.
- Ask children to tell you what letter to start *Mark* with as you write it down on the board or easel pad. Invite volunteers to come up and write the remaining letters using their phonics skills to match sounds and letters.
- Have children use their own paper to practice writing the letters in the word *Mark*.
- Use a similar procedure for the word *Kirk* in the second blank in the sentence.
- When you are finished, display the chart page and invite children to make comparisons between the words *Mark* and *Kirk* on the chart page and the same words on their own papers. Going back to the original print encourages children to use print resources in their spelling.

Using Word Wall Starters

- **Song Chart Word** Display the word *large* from the Word Wall Starters pack. Ask if anyone recognizes the word. Compare the word to *large* on the chart page. Invite children to tell you what letters are highlighted in yellow on each card. Use the *vowels with r* label to start this section of your Word Wall and place the card *large* beneath it. Be sure to group *r*-controlled vowels with the same letters together. Later as children encounter additional *r*-controlled vowels in their reading and other class work, write each new word on an index card and highlight the *r*-controlled vowel. Add these words to this section of your Word Wall as well.
- **Big Book Word** After you have read the Big Book *Barge Cat*, display the word *barge* from the Word Wall Starters pack. Using the word card and the Big Book, use a routine similar to the one above, and place the word card *barge* beneath the other *r*-controlled vowel words with *ar*.

Assessment for STAGES

❶❷ Although these children may participate in *r*-controlled vowel instruction, they should not be expected to master or apply it.

❸ Say the word *Mark* and have the child point to the word on the chart page. Identify the letters *ar* together and underline them with your finger. Invite him or her to identify which of the following words also has *ar*: *light, star, road*. As desired, use a similar routine for *ir, er,* and *or*.

❹❺ Say the word *Mark* and have the child point to the word on the chart page. Ask him or her to identify the letters *ar* and underline them with a finger. Have the child think of another word that has *ar* in it. If he or she needs assistance, sing the song together and encourage the child to identify a word in the song. As desired, use a similar routine for *ir, er,* and *or*.

Take-Home Phonics Story

Reading the Book in Class
- Distribute copies of pages 55–56 from the Take-Home Phonics Stories. Have children create their own books.
- For Emergent readers, read one of the books created by a child to a small group of four to six children one or more times. For Early readers, you can skip this step.
- Invite children to buddy read the book in pairs of heterogeneous stages.
- As they seem ready, have children read the book independently.

Connecting to Home
- Tell children to take the books they made home to share with their families once they are able to read them independently.
- Be sure to include the Parent Letter from pages 3–10 of the Take-Home Phonics Stories in the appropriate home language when you send home the book made by each child.

Phonics Song Chart 23   Words with R-Controlled Vowels

Initial Blends *cl* and *pl*

Setting the Scene

- Bring in some plums for the class to taste. Ask children if they ever tasted a plum before. Allow children to share their experiences. Before snacking on the plums, hold one up and tell children that plums are a kind of juicy fruit that grow on trees and that they are usually purple. Then give a plum to each child to enjoy! Remind children not to eat the pits.

Creating Comprehensible Input

- Say the chant slowly as you use gestures and pointing to make it comprehensible.

Climb the tree. Pick some plums.	make a climbing motion, then act out picking a plum
Climb the tree. Pick some plums.	make a climbing motion, then act out picking a plum
Let's clean all the plums.	make a cleaning motion with your hands
We can hardly wait.	pretend to cheer
Pile the plums on a platter or plate.	point to the platter of plums
There are plenty of plums.	point to several plums on the platter
They will taste so great.	rub your stomach and smile
Climb the tree. Pick some plums.	make a climbing motion, then act out picking a plum

Singing and Gestures

- Sing the song together as you play it on the Phonics Audio CD. Once they learn the song, teach children gestures they can make as they sing it again.
- Ask children to pretend they are climbing a ladder to pick some plums as they sing the first, second, and last lines of the song.
- Invite children to act out the rest of the song as they sing it, such as picking and cleaning the plums, piling them on a platter, and eating them!

Recognizing Words with *cl* and *pl* Initial Blends

- Sing the first line of the song, then point to the word *Climb* as you say it. Write it on the board or easel pad and say the word again. Point to the letters *Cl* and tell children that the letters stand for the beginning sounds they hear in *Climb*. Ask if they can find another word that begins like *Climb*. [*clean*] Write the word *clean* under the word *Climb*. Tell children that there are many words that begin with /cl/. Ask volunteers for any other words they can think of that begin with *cl*. Bear in mind that only children in Stages 3–5 will be able to brainstorm English words based on sounds.
- Invite children to pretend they are climbing a ladder each time they hear /cl/ as you say the following words: *clip, take, clue, clap, snap, class, friend, clam, clear, drive.*
- Use a similar routine for words that begin with *pl*.

Chart 24 — Sung to the tune of "Three Blind Mice"

Climb the tree. Pick some plums.
Climb the tree. Pick some plums.
Let's clean all the plums.
We can hardly wait.
Pile the plums on a platter or plate.
There are plenty of plums.
They will taste so great.
Climb the tree. Pick some plums.

Language Junction

Some languages, including Cantonese and Vietnamese, lack consonant blends. As a result, some Cantonese- and Vietnamese-speaking children may initially find it challenging to pronounce consonant blends in English. Some of these learners may tend to insert a short vowel sound between the consonants or, in some cases, to eliminate one of the consonants.

STAGES: ① Preproduction ② Early Production ③ Speech Emergence ④ Intermediate Fluency ⑤ Advanced Fluency

Exploring Sound-Symbol Relationships

- Use small sticky notes to cover up the last letters of each word on the chart page that begins with *cl* or *pl*. This will encourage children to focus on the print of *cl* and *pl*.
- After removing the sticky notes, invite children to come up to the chart page and practice underlining the letters that make /cl/ and /pl/ with their fingers.

Writing Words with *cl* and *pl* Initial Blends

- Encourage children to use their phonics skills in writing. Put away the chart page and write the following sentence on the board or easel pad:

  Let's _____ all the _____.

- Ask volunteers to tell you what goes in the first blank. Invite the group to say the word *clean* together, stretching the sounds.
- Ask children to tell you what letter to start *clean* with as you write it down on the board or easel pad. Invite volunteers to come up and write the remaining letters.
- Have children use their own paper to practice writing the letters in the word *clean*.
- Use a similar procedure for the word *plums* in the second blank in the sentence.
- When you are finished, display the chart page and invite children to make comparisons between the words *clean* and *plums* on the chart page and the same words on their own papers.

Using Word Wall Starters

- **Song Chart Words** Display the words *climb*, *clean*, and *plate* from the Word Wall Starters pack. Ask if anyone recognizes the words. Compare the words to *Climb*, *clean*, and *plate* on the chart page. Invite children to tell you what letters are highlighted in yellow on each card. Use the *cl* and *pl* labels to start the *cl* and *pl* initial blend sections of your Word Wall and place the cards *climb*, *clean*, and *plate* beneath them. Later as children encounter additional *cl* and *pl* initial blends in their reading and other class work, write each new word on an index card and highlight the blend. Add these words to this section of your Word Wall as well.
- **Big Book Word** After you have read the Big Book *Barge Cat*, display the word *plank* from the Word Wall Starters pack. Use a routine similar to the one above, and place the word card *plank* beneath the other words that begin with *pl*.

Assessment for STAGES

❶❷ Although these children may participate in initial blend instruction, they should not be expected to master or apply it.

❸ Say the word *Climb* and have the child point to the word on the chart page. Identify the letters *cl* together and underline them with your finger. Invite him or her to identify which of the following words also begins with the *cl* initial blend: *tap, snap, clap*. As desired, use a similar routine for the *pl* initial blend.

❹❺ Say the word *Climb* and have the child point to the word on the chart page. Ask him or her to identify the letters *cl* and underline them with a finger. Have the child think of another word that begins with /cl/. If he or she needs assistance, sing the song together and encourage the child to identify a word in the song. As desired, use a similar routine for the *pl* initial blend.

Take-Home Phonics Story

Reading the Book in Class

- Distribute copies of pages 57–58 from the Take-Home Phonics Stories. Have children create their own books.
- For Emergent readers, read one of the books created by a child to a small group of four to six children one or more times. For Early readers, you can skip this step.
- Invite children to buddy read the book in pairs of heterogeneous stages.
- As they seem ready, have children read the book independently.

Word Bank

cl	pl
clap	place
class	plane
claw	plant
clay	platter
clean	play
cliff	please
clip	plenty
close	pluck
cloud	plum
clown	plus

Connecting to Home

- Tell children to take the books they made home to share with their families once they are able to read them independently.
- Be sure to include the Parent Letter from pages 3–10 of the Take-Home Phonics Stories in the appropriate home language when you send home the book made by each child.

Phonics Song Chart 24   Initial Blends *cl* and *pl*   **P53**

It just snowed, so grab your sled.
Put your black hat on your head.
Zip your coat because the wind will blow.
Please don't slip. Watch where you go!
Slide down the slope on your
 big blue sled.
Watch out for blocks of ice ahead!

CHART 25
Sung to the tune of "Hush, Little Baby"

Extending to the *fl* Initial Blend

Sung to the tune of
 "Hush, Little Baby"
Watch the flock of birds take
 flight.
When they fly, it's quite a sight!
Watch their wings flap as they
 fly.
Watch the flock up in the sky.

Language Junction

Although Hmong does have consonant blends, the initial blend *sl* doesn't exist in the language. As a result, some Hmong-speaking children may have difficulty producing the sound. In addition, /bl/ is spelled differently in Hmong. As a result, there may be some negative transfer, and children who know Hmong print may initially decode the English letters *bl* with the sound from their home language.

Initial Blends *sl* and *bl*

Setting the Scene

- Ask children if they have ever seen snow. Explain that in certain places that are cold, it will snow. Bring in a picture of a sled or a real sled, if possible. Ask children if they have ever been sledding. Allow them to share their experiences.

Creating Comprehensible Input

- Say the chant slowly as you use gestures and pointing to make it comprehensible.

It just snowed, so grab your sled.	make a motion with your hands indicating falling snow, then point to the sled
Put your black hat on your head.	point to the black hat, then act out putting a hat on your head
Zip your coat because the wind will blow.	act out zipping your coat, then wave your hands to show *wind*
Please don't slip. Watch where you go!	act out slipping
Slide down the slope on your big blue sled.	point to the hill, then to the sled
Watch out for blocks of ice ahead!	hold your hand up to your forehead

Singing and Gestures

- Sing the song together as you play it on the Phonics Audio CD. Once they learn the song, teach children gestures they can make to go along with it.
- Whenever they sing *sled*, have children act out sledding down a hill.
- Invite children to act out the rest of the song as they sing the actions: putting their hats on, zipping up their coats, walking slowly and carefully, and watching for ice.

Recognizing Words with *sl* and *bl* Initial Blends

- Sing the first line of the song, then point to the word *sled* as you say it. Write it on the board or easel pad and say the word again. Point to the letters *sl* and tell children that the letters stand for the beginning sounds they hear in *sled*. Ask if they can find any other words that begin like *sled*. [slip, Slide, slope] Write these words under the word *sled*. Tell children that there are many words that begin with /sl/. Ask volunteers for any other words they can think of that begin with *sl*. Bear in mind that only children in Stages 3–5 will be able to brainstorm English words based on sounds.
- Invite children to pretend they are sitting on a sled each time they hear /sl/ as you say the following words: *slip, walk, slice, cut, fast, slow, wake, sleep, slim, bug*.
- Continue a similar routine for words that begin with the *bl* blend.

Exploring Sound-Symbol Relationships

- Use small sticky notes to cover up the last letters of each word on the chart page that begins with *sl* or *bl*. This will encourage children to focus on the print of *sl* and *bl*.
- After removing the sticky notes, invite children to come up to the chart page and practice underlining the letters that make /sl/ and /bl/ with their fingers.

STAGES ① Preproduction ② Early Production ③ Speech Emergence ④ Intermediate Fluency ⑤ Advanced Fluency

Writing Words with *sl* and *bl* Initial Blends

- Encourage children to use their phonics skills in writing. Put away the chart page and write the following sentence on the board or easel pad:
  Slide down the _____ on your big _____ sled.
- Ask volunteers to tell you what goes in the first blank. Invite the group to say *slope* together, stretching the sounds.
- Ask children to tell you what letter to start *slope* with as you write it down on the board or easel pad. Invite volunteers to come up and write the remaining letters using their phonics skills to match sounds and letters.
- Have children use their own paper to practice writing the letters in the word *slope*.
- Use a similar procedure for the word *blue* in the second blank in the sentence.
- When you are finished, display the chart page and invite children to make comparisons between the words *slope* and *blue* on the chart page and the same words on their own papers. Going back to the original print encourages children to use print resources in their spelling.

Using Word Wall Starters

- **Song Chart Words** Display the words *sled*, *black*, and *blue* from the Word Wall Starters pack. Ask if anyone recognizes the words. Compare the words to *sled*, *black*, and *blue* on the chart page. Invite children to tell you what letters are highlighted in yellow on each card. Use the *sl* and *bl* labels to start the *sl* and *bl* initial blend sections of your Word Wall and place the cards *sled*, *black*, and *blue* beneath them. Later as children encounter additional *sl* and *bl* initial blends in their reading and other class work, write each new word on an index card and highlight the blend. Add these words to this section of your Word Wall as well.
- **Big Book Word** After you have read the Big Book *Barge Cat*, display the word *slowly* from the Word Wall Starters pack. Using the word card and the Big Book, use a routine similar to the one above, and place the word card *slowly* beneath the other words that begin with *sl*.

Assessment for STAGES

❶❷ Although these children may participate in initial blend instruction, they should not be expected to master or apply it.

❸ Say the word *sled* and have the child point to the word on the chart page. Identify the letters *sl* together and underline them with your finger. Invite him or her to identify which of the following words also begins with the *sl* blend: *hop*, *dance*, *slide*. As desired, use a similar routine for the *bl* initial blend.

❹❺ Say the word *sled* and have the child point to the word on the chart page. Ask him or her to identify the letters *sl* and underline them with a finger. Have the child think of another word that begins with /sl/. If he or she needs assistance, sing the song together and encourage the child to identify a word in the song. As desired, use a similar routine for the *bl* initial blend.

Take-Home Phonics Story

Reading the Book in Class
- Distribute copies of pages 59–60 from the Take-Home Phonics Stories. Have children create their own books.
- For Emergent readers, read one of the books created by a child to a small group of four to six children one or more times. For Early readers, you can skip this step.
- Invite children to buddy read the book in pairs of heterogeneous stages.
- As they seem ready, have children read the book independently.

Word Bank

sl	bl
sled	black
sleep	blame
slide	blast
slip	block
slot	blow
slow	blue

Connecting to Home

- Tell children to take the books they made home to share with their families once they are able to read them independently.
- Be sure to include the Parent Letter from pages 3–10 of the Take-Home Phonics Stories in the appropriate home language when you send home the book made by each child.

Phonics Song Chart 25   Initial Blends *sl* and *bl*   **P55**

Oh, Greg and Tray took a
trip today
Trip today
Trip today.
Oh, Greg and Tray took a
trip today
To see Grandma Grace!

CHART 26
Sung to the tune of "The Wheels on the Bus"

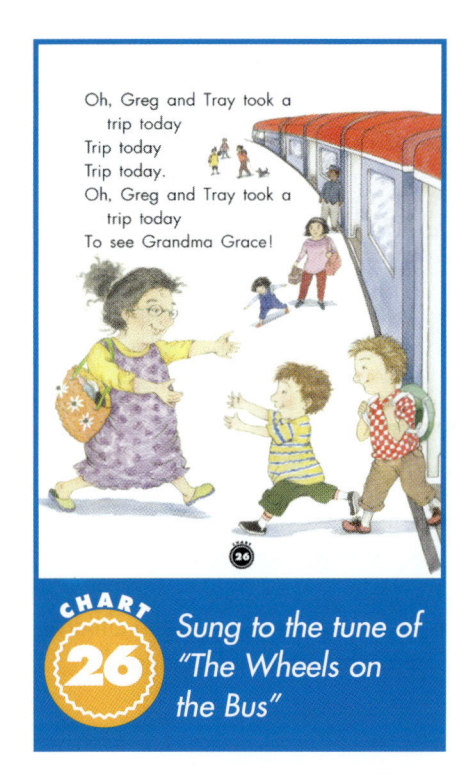

Extending to the dr Initial Blend

Sung to the tune of "The Wheels on the Bus"
I drank juice and made a mess,
made a mess, on my dress.
I now will fill my cup with less,
so my dress stays dry!

Language Junction

Khmer does not have a *g* sound, so blends with *g* may be especially challenging for Khmer-speaking children to produce. In addition, speakers of Arabic may have difficulty producing the initial blend *gr*, because the combination does not exist in their language.

P56

Initial Blends *gr* and *tr*

Setting the Scene
- Bring in a small suitcase from home. Ask children if they have ever gone on a trip to visit a friend or a family member. Allow children to share their experiences. Then ask if they have ever ridden on a train. Bring in a pictures of trains as you explain this kind of transportation.

Creating Comprehensible Input
- Say the chant slowly as you use gestures and pointing to make it comprehensible.

Oh, Greg and Tray took a trip today	point to the two boys, then hold up the suitcase
Trip today	hold up the suitcase
Trip today.	hold up the suitcase
Oh, Greg and Tray took a trip today	point to the two boys, then hold up the suitcase
To see Grandma Grace!	point to the boys' grandma

Singing and Gestures
- Sing the song together as you play it on the Phonics Audio CD. Once they learn the song, teach children gestures they can make to go along with it.
- Each time children sing the word *trip*, have them pretend they are holding a suitcase.
- On the last line of the song, have children wave as they pretend to see Grandma Grace!

Recognizing Words with *gr* and *tr* Initial Blends
- Sing the first line of the song, then point to the word *Greg* as you say it. Write it on the board or easel pad and say the word again. Point to the letters *Gr* and tell children that the letters stand for the beginning sounds they hear in *Greg*. Ask if they can find any other words that begin like *Greg*. [*Grandma, Grace*] Write these words under the word *Greg*. Tell children that there are many words that begin with /gr/. Ask volunteers for any other words they can think of that begin with /gr/. Bear in mind that only children in Stages 3–5 will be able to brainstorm English words based on sounds.
- Invite children to pretend they are waving to Grandma Grace each time they hear /gr/ as you say the following words: *groan, laugh, banana, grape, touch, grab, great, small, group, meet*.
- Use a similar routine for words that begin with the *tr* blend.

Exploring Sound-Symbol Relationships
- Use small sticky notes to cover up the last letters of each word on the chart page that begins with *gr* or *tr*. This will encourage children to focus on the print of *gr* and *tr*.
- After removing the sticky notes, invite children to come up to the chart page and practice underlining the letters that make /gr/ and /tr/ with their fingers.

STAGES ① Preproduction ② Early Production ③ Speech Emergence ④ Intermediate Fluency ⑤ Advanced Fluency

Writing Words with *gr* and *tr* Initial Blends

- Encourage children to use their phonics skills in writing. Put away the chart page and write the following sentence on the board or easel pad:

    Oh, _____ and Tray took a _____ today.
- Ask volunteers to tell you what goes in the first blank. Invite the group to say the word *Greg* together, stretching the sounds.
- Ask children to tell you what letter to start *Greg* with as you write it down on the board or easel pad. Invite volunteers to come up and write the remaining letters using their phonics skills to match sounds and letters.
- Have children use their own paper to practice writing the letters in the word *Greg*.
- Use a similar procedure for the word *trip* in the second blank in the sentence.
- When you are finished, display the chart page and invite children to make comparisons between the words *Greg* and *trip* on the chart page and the same words on their own papers. Going back to the original print encourages children to use print resources in their spelling.

Using Word Wall Starters

- **Song Chart Words** Display the words *Greg*, *Grandma*, and *trip* from the Word Wall Starters pack. Ask if anyone recognizes the words. Compare the words to *Greg*, *Grandma*, and *trip* on the chart page. Invite children to tell you what letters are highlighted in yellow on each card. Use the *gr* and *tr* labels to start the *gr* and *tr* initial blend sections of your Word Wall and place the cards *Greg*, *Grandma*, and *trip* beneath them. Later as children encounter additional *gr* and *tr* initial blends in their reading and other class work, write each new word on an index card and highlight the blend. Add these words to this section of your Word Wall as well.
- **Big Book Word** After you have read the Big Book *How Bicycles Work*, display the word *trails* from the Word Wall Starters pack. Using the word card and the Big Book, use a routine similar to the one above, and place the word card *trails* beneath the other words that begin with *tr*.

Assessment for STAGES

❶❷ Although these children may participate in initial blend instruction, they should not be expected to master or apply it.

❸ Say the word *Greg* and have the child point to the word on the chart page. Identify the letters *Gr* together and underline them with your finger. Invite him or her to identify which of the following words also begins with the *gr* initial blend: *whistle, talk, groan*. As desired, use a similar routine for words that begin with the *tr* blend.

❹❺ Say the word *Greg* and have the child point to the word on the chart page. Ask him or her to identify the letters *Gr* and underline them with a finger. Have the child think of another word that begins with /gr/. If he or she needs assistance, sing the song together and encourage the child to identify a word in the song. As desired, use a similar routine for words beginning with /tr/.

Take-Home Phonics Story

Reading the Book in Class
- Distribute copies of pages 61–62 from the Take-Home Phonics Stories. Have children create their own books.
- For Emergent readers, read one of the books created by a child to a small group of four to six children one or more times. For Early readers, you can skip this step.
- Invite children to buddy read the book in pairs of heterogeneous stages.
- As they seem ready, have children read the book independently.

Word Bank

gr	tr
grab	track
grade	tractor
grand	trade
grant	trail
grape	train
grass	trap
gray	trash
great	travel
green	tray
grin	treat

Connecting to Home

- Tell children to take the books they made home to share with their families once they are able to read them independently.
- Be sure to include the Parent Letter from pages 3–10 of the Take-Home Phonics Stories in the appropriate home language when you send home the book made by each child.

Phonics Song Chart 26   Initial Blends gr and tr   **P57**

CHART 27 — Sung to the tune of "If You're Happy"

Bravo's brownies win first prize at the fair.
Bravo's brownies win first prize at the fair.
Bravo brings them on a plate.
He is proud that they taste great!
Bravo's brownies win first prize at the fair.

Extending to the *cr* and *fr* Initial Blends

Sung to the tune of "If You're Happy"
Every Friday I eat crackers and fresh fruit.
Every Friday I eat crackers and fresh fruit.
I do love each crispy cracker.
Every Friday I'm a snacker!
Every Friday I eat crackers and fresh fruit.

Language Junction

Speakers of Cantonese, which lacks consonant blends, may find it challenging to pronounce blends with *r*. They may insert a vowel sound to break up the blends, making /pr/ sound like the word *per*. Or, some speakers may substitute /l/ for /r/ in initial consonant blends.

Initial Blends *br* and *pr*

Setting the Scene
- Bring in some brownies that you've made or bought. Tell children that they will be making place mats for some special treats. Have materials available, such as multi-colored construction paper, glitter, ribbons, scissors, glue, and so on. When children are done, hold up each place mat and talk about why it is special. Tell children that you have a prize to give each of them for making their terrific place mats—a brownie!

Creating Comprehensible Input
- Say the chant slowly as you use gestures and pointing to make it comprehensible.

Bravo's brownies win first prize at the fair.	point to the boy, then to the brownies, then to his ribbon
Bravo's brownies win first prize at the fair.	point to the boy, then to the brownies, then to his ribbon
Bravo brings them on a plate.	point to the boy, then to the plate of brownies
He is proud that they taste great!	put your hands on your hips, then rub your stomach
Bravo's brownies win first prize at the fair.	point to the boy, then to the brownies, then to his ribbon

Singing and Gestures
- Sing the song together as you play it on the Phonics Audio CD. Once they learn the song, teach children gestures they can make to go along with it.
- Each time children sing the word *brownies*, have them make a square with their hands, indicating a big brownie square.
- When children sing *first prize*, have them hold up one finger in the air.
- As children sing *taste great*, have them rub their stomachs!

Recognizing Words with *br* and *pr* Initial Blends
- Sing the first line of the song, then point to the word *Bravo's* as you say it. Write it on the board or easel pad and say the word again. Point to the letters *Br* and tell children that the letters stand for the beginning sounds they hear in *Bravo's*. Ask if they can find another word that begins like *Bravo's*. [brownies, Bravo, brings] Write these words under the word *Bravo's*. Tell children that there are many words that begin with /br/. Ask volunteers for any other words they can think of that begin with *br*. Bear in mind that only children in Stages 3–5 will be able to brainstorm English words based on sounds.
- Invite children to pretend to take a bite of brownie each time they hear /br/ as you say the following words: *bring, take, bright, dark, fix, break, river, bridge, breeze, pot*.
- Use a similar routine for words that begin with the *pr* blend.

Exploring Sound-Symbol Relationships
- Use small sticky notes to cover up the last letters of each word on the chart page that begins with *br* or *pr*. This will encourage children to focus on the print of *br* and *pr*.
- After removing the sticky notes, invite children to come up to the chart page and practice underlining the letters that make /br/ and /pr/ with their fingers.

STAGES ❶ Preproduction ❷ Early Production ❸ Speech Emergence ❹ Intermediate Fluency ❺ Advanced Fluency

Writing Words with *br* and *pr* Initial Blends

- Encourage children to use their phonics skills in writing. Put away the chart page and write the following sentence on the board or easel pad:
    Bravo's _____ win first _____ at the fair.
- Ask volunteers to tell you what goes in the first blank. Invite the group to say the word *brownies* together, stretching the sounds.
- Ask children to tell you what letter to start *brownies* with as you write it down on the board or easel pad. Invite volunteers to come up and write the remaining letters using their phonics skills to match sounds and letters.
- Have children use their own paper to practice writing the letters in the word *brownies*.
- Use a similar procedure for the word *prize* in the second blank.
- When you are finished, display the chart page and invite children to make comparisons between the words *brownies* and *prize* on the chart page and the same words on their own papers. Going back to the original print encourages children to use print resources in their spelling.

Using Word Wall Starters

- **Song Chart Words** Display the words *brownies*, *prize*, and *proud* from the Word Wall Starters pack. Ask if anyone recognizes the words. Compare the words to *brownies*, *prize*, and *proud* on the chart page. Invite children to tell you what letters are highlighted in yellow on each card. Use the *br* and *pr* labels to start the *br* and *pr* initial blend sections of your Word Wall and place the cards *brownies*, *prize*, and *proud* beneath the appropriate label. Later as children encounter additional *br* and *pr* blends in their reading and other class work, write each new word on an index card and highlight the blend. Add these words to the appropriate sections of your Word Wall as well.
- **Big Book Word** After you have read the Big Book *How Bicycles Work*, display the word *brake* from the Word Wall Starters pack. Using the word card and the Big Book, use a routine similar to the one above, and place the card *brake* beneath the other words that begin with *br*.

Assessment for STAGES

❶❷ Although these children may participate in initial blend instruction, they should not be expected to master or apply it.

❸ Say the word *Bravo's* and have the child point to the word on the chart page. Identify the letters *Br* together and underline them with your finger. Invite him or her to identify which of the following words also begins with the initial *br* blend: *bun, bread, cake*. As desired, use a similar routine for words that begin with the *pr* blend.

❹❺ Say the word *Bravo's* and have the child point to the word on the chart page. Ask him or her to identify the letters *Br* and underline them with a finger. Have the child think of another word that begins with /br/. If he or she needs assistance, sing the song together and encourage the child to identify a word in the song. As desired, use a similar routine for words beginning with /pr/.

Take-Home Phonics Story

Reading the Book in Class
- Distribute copies of pages 63–64 from the Take-Home Phonics Stories. Have children create their own books.
- For Emergent readers, read one of the books created by a child to a small group of four to six children one or more times. For Early readers, you can skip this step.
- Invite children to buddy read the book in pairs of heterogeneous stages.
- As they seem ready, have children read the book independently.

Word Bank

br	pr
brake	price
branch	prince
brand	princess
brass	print
brave	prize
Bravo	problem
bread	promise
bridge	proud
brings	prove
brownies	prowl

Connecting to Home

- Tell children to take the books they made home to share with their families once they are able to read them independently.
- Be sure to include the Parent Letter from pages 3–10 of the Take-Home Phonics Stories in the appropriate home language when you send home the book made by each child.

Phonics Song Chart 27   Initial Blends *br* and *pr*

Initial Blends *st* and *sk*

Setting the Scene

- Show children a picture of a skunk and say *skunk*, asking them to echo you. Explain that skunks are bushy-tailed animals that are black with white stripes running down their backs. Mention that when skunks get scared, they squirt a liquid that smells terrible. Ask children if they have ever seen or smelled a skunk. Allow them to share their experiences. Warn children not to get too close to skunks.

Creating Comprehensible Input

- Say the chant slowly as you use gestures and pointing to make it comprehensible.

First I stop to stare at a skinny skunk!	point to your eyes, then point to the skunk
He sits on top of an old tree trunk.	pretend to sit down, then point to the tree trunk
Then I stay and watch him start to eat.	point to yourself, then point to the acorns
I will name him Skinny Pete!	point to yourself, then point to the words *Skinny Pete*

Singing and Gestures

- Sing the song together as you play it on the Phonics Audio CD. Once they learn the song, teach children gestures they can make as they sing it again.
- Each time they sing the word *I*, have them to point to themselves.
- Have them point to their eyes when they sing the words *stare* and *watch*.
- Children can act out sitting for *sits* in line two.

Recognizing Words with *st* and *sk* Initial Blends

- Sing the first line of the song, then point to the word *stop* as you say it. Write it on the board or easel pad and say the word again. Point to the letters *st* and tell children that the letters stand for the beginning sounds they hear in *stop*. Ask if they can find any other words that begin like stop. [*stare, stay, start*] Write these words under the word *stop*. Tell children that there are many words that begin with /st/. Ask volunteers for any other words they can think of that begin with *st*. Bear in mind that only children in Stages 3–5 will be able to brainstorm English words based on sounds.
- Invite children to point to act out sitting each time they hear /st/ as you say the following words: *stick, stamp, tap, stone, fold, stew, pot, star, step, in*.
- Use a similar routine for words that begin with the *sk* blend.

Exploring Sound-Symbol Relationships

- Use small sticky notes to cover up the last letters of each word on the chart page that begins with *st* or *sk*. This will encourage children to focus on the print of *st* and *sk*.
- After removing the sticky notes, invite children to come up to the chart page and practice underlining the letters that make /st/ and /sk/ with their fingers.

CHART 28

Sung to the tune of "I'm a Little Teapot"

First I stop to stare at a skinny skunk!
He sits on top of an old tree trunk.
Then I stay and watch him start to eat.
I will name him Skinny Pete!

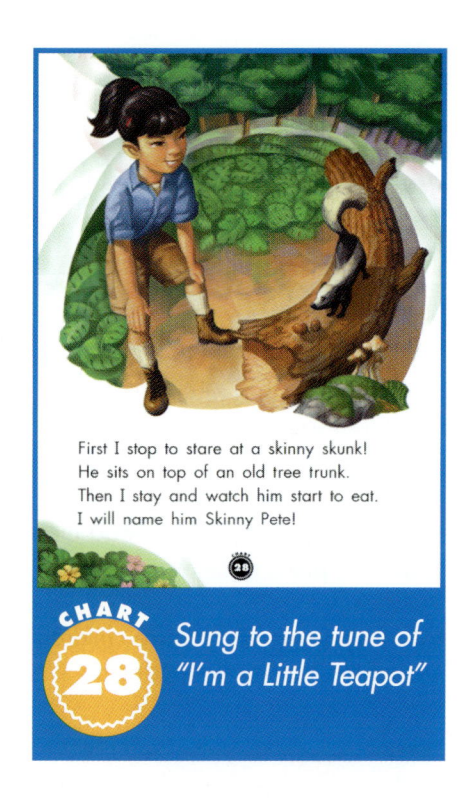

Extending to the *sp* Initial Blend

Sung to the tune of "I'm a Little Teapot"

I spy special things. It's Saturday.
I spy my friends playing sports today.
I spy lots of children running by.
I spy a kite spinning in the sky.

Language Junction

Consonant blends with /s/ do not occur at the beginning of words in Spanish. As a result, some children whose home language is Spanish may tend to add a vowel sound before the *s* sound in English words beginning with *s* blends. For example, they may make a vowel sound at the beginning of words like *stay, skate,* or *school*. One tip to help these children is to have them stretch out the *s* sound before they pronounce the *st* or *sk* blend.

P60

STAGES ① Preproduction ② Early Production ③ Speech Emergence ④ Intermediate Fluency ⑤ Advanced Fluency

Writing Words with *st* and *sk* Initial Blends

- Encourage children to use their phonics skills in writing. Put away the chart page and write the following sentence on the board or easel pad:
  First I _____ to stare at a skinny _____ !
- Ask volunteers to tell you what goes in the first blank. Invite the group to say the word *stop* together, stretching the sounds.
- Ask children to tell you what letter to start *stop* with as you write it down on the board or easel pad. Invite volunteers to come up and write the remaining letters using their phonics skills to match sounds and letters.
- Have children use their own paper to practice writing the letters in the word *stop*.
- Use a similar procedure for the word *skunk* in the second blank in the sentence.
- When you are finished, display the chart page and invite children to make comparisons between the words *stop* and *skunk* on the chart page and the same words on their own papers. Going back to the original print encourages children to use print resources in their spelling.

Using Word Wall Starters

- **Song Chart Words** Display the words *stay*, *skinny*, and *skunk* from the Word Wall Starters pack. Ask if anyone recognizes the words. Compare the words to *stay*, *skinny*, and *skunk* on the chart page. Invite children to tell you what letters are highlighted in yellow on each card. Use the *st* and *sk* labels to start the *st* and *sk* initial blend sections of your Word Wall and place the cards *stay*, *skinny*, and *skunk* beneath the appropriate label. Later as children encounter additional *st* and *sk* initial blends in their reading and other class work, write each new word on an index card and highlight the blend. Add these words to the appropriate sections of your Word Wall as well.
- **Big Book Word** After you have read the Big Book *How Bicycles Work*, display the word *stop* from the Word Wall Starters pack. Using the word card and the Big Book, use a routine similar to the one above, and place the word card *stop* beneath the other words that begin with *st*.

Assessment for STAGES

① ② Although these children may participate in initial blend instruction, they should not be expected to master or apply it.

③ Say the word *stop* and have the child point to the word on the chart page. Identify the letters *st* together and underline them with your finger. Invite him or her to identify which of the following words also begins with the *st* initial blend: *market*, *shop*, *store*. As desired, use a similar routine for words that begin with the *sk* blend.

④ ⑤ Say the word *stop* and have the child point to the word on the chart page. Ask him or her to identify the letters *st* and underline them with a finger. Have the child think of another word that begins with /st/. If he or she needs assistance, sing the song together and encourage the child to identify a word in the song. As desired, use a similar routine for words beginning with /sk/.

Take-Home Phonics Story

Reading the Book in Class
- Distribute copies of pages 65–66 from the Take-Home Phonics Stories. Have children create their own books.
- For Emergent readers, read one of the books created by a child to a small group of four to six children one or more times. For Early readers, you can skip this step.
- Invite children to buddy read the book in pairs of heterogeneous stages.
- As they seem ready, have children read the book independently.

Word Bank

st	sk
stand	skate
star	skateboard
stare	skeleton
start	sketch
stay	skin
steam	skinny
stop	skip
storm	skunk
store	sky
story	skyline

Connecting to Home

- Tell children to take the books they made home to share with their families once they are able to read them independently.
- Be sure to include the Parent Letter from pages 3–10 of the Take-Home Phonics Stories in the appropriate home language when you send home the book made by each child.

Phonics Song Chart 28   Initial Blends st and sk

We see small swans
swimming in the big pond.
We smile sweetly
when they swim past us.

CHART 29 Sung to the tune of "Alouette"

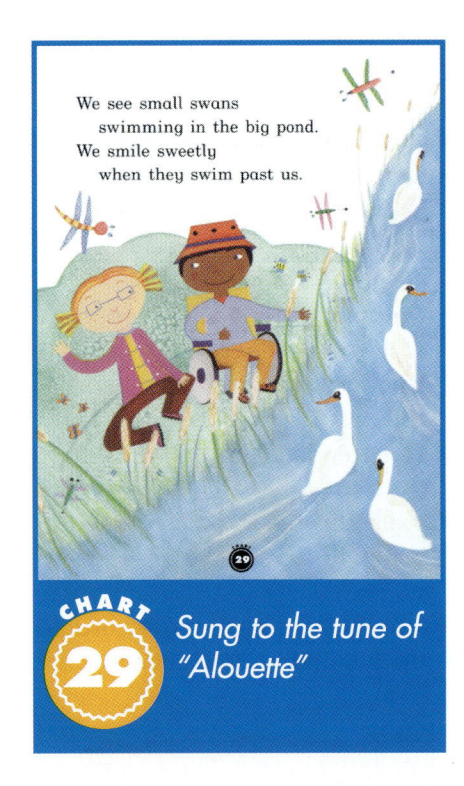

Extending to the sn Initial Blend

Sung to the tune of
"Alouette"
We have snacks, then
  go play in the wet snow.
We make snowballs.
We throw them high and low.

Language Junction

Korean learners of English may find it a challenge to produce blends in English at the beginning or end of words. They may tend to insert a vowel between the consonants to break up the consonant blends. Blends with /s/ may be particularly difficult for them as the sound does not exist in Korean.

Initial Blends *sw* and *sm*

Setting the Scene

- Bring in a picture book of water birds that includes swans. Explain that swans are graceful birds with long, curvy necks. As you say *curvy*, trace the picture of a swan's neck. Mention that adult swans are usually white.
- Have children pretend they are graceful swans, swimming in the water. Encourage them to stretch their necks as high as they can.

Creating Comprehensible Input

- Say the chant slowly as you use gestures and pointing to make it comprehensible.

| We see small swans swimming in the big pond. | hold your hand up to your forehead, point to the swans, then point to the pond |
| We smile sweetly when they swim past us. | smile, then make the shape of a swan's neck with your arm and shuffle forward |

Singing and Gestures

- Sing the song together as you play it on the Phonics Audio CD. Once they learn the song, teach children gestures they can make as they sing it again.
- Split the class into two groups. Have the members of one group pretend they are sitting on the side of the pond, watching and smiling at the swans. Invite the members of the other group to pretend to be swans by making the shape of a swan's neck with their arms and shuffling forward. Allow groups to switch roles.

Recognizing Words with *sw* and *sm* Initial Blends

- Sing the first line of the song, then point to the word *small* as you say it. Write it on the board or easel pad and say the word again. Point to the letters *sm* and tell children that the letters stand for the beginning sounds they hear in *small*. Ask if they can find another word that begins like *small*. [*smile*] Write the word *smile* under the word *small*. Tell children that there are many words that begin with /sm/. Ask volunteers for any other words they can think of that begin with *sm*. Bear in mind that only children in Stages 3–5 will be able to brainstorm English words based on sounds.
- Invite children to smile each time they hear /sm/ as you say the following words: *smell, rose, smart, eyes, rough, smooth, fire, smoke, bell, smash*.
- Use a similar routine for words that begin with the *sw* blend.

Exploring Sound-Symbol Relationships

- Use small sticky notes to cover up the last letters of each word on the chart page that begins with *sw* or *sm*. This will encourage children to focus on the print of *sw* and *sm*.
- After removing the sticky notes, invite children to come up to the chart page and practice underlining the letters that make /sw/ and /sm/ with their fingers.

STAGES ① Preproduction ② Early Production ③ Speech Emergence ④ Intermediate Fluency ⑤ Advanced Fluency

Writing Words with *sw* and *sm* Initial Blends

- Encourage children to use their phonics skills in writing. Put away the chart page and write the following sentence on the board or easel pad:

    We see _____ _____ swimming in the big pond.

- Ask volunteers to tell you what goes in the first blank. Invite the group to say the word *small* together, stretching the sounds.
- Ask children to tell you what letter to start *small* with as you write it down on the board or easel pad. Invite volunteers to come up and write the remaining letters using their phonics skills to match sounds and letters.
- Have children use their own paper to practice writing the letters in the word *small*.
- Use a similar procedure for the word *swans* in the second blank in the sentence.
- When you are finished, display the chart page and invite children to make comparisons between the words *small* and *swans* on the chart page and the same words on their own papers. Going back to the original print encourages children to use print resources in their spelling.

Using Word Wall Starters

- **Song Chart Words** Display the words *swans*, *swim*, and *smile* from the Word Wall Starters pack. Ask if anyone recognizes the words. Compare the words to *swans*, *swim*, and *smile* on the chart page. Invite children to tell you what letters are highlighted in yellow on each card. Use the *sw* and *sm* labels to start the *sw* and *sm* initial blend sections of your Word Wall and place the cards *swans*, *swim*, and *smile* beneath the appropriate label. Later as children encounter additional *sw* and *sm* initial blends in their reading and other class work, write each new word on an index card and highlight the blend. Add the words to the appropriate sections of your Word Wall as well.
- **Big Book Word** After you have read the Big Book *How Bicycles Work*, display the word *small* from the Word Wall Starters pack. Using the word card and the Big Book, use a routine similar to the one above, and place the word card *small* beneath the other words that begin with *sm*.

Assessment for STAGES

❶❷ Although these children may participate in word family instruction, they should not be expected to master or apply it.

❸ Say the word *swans* and have the child point to the word on the chart page. Identify the letters *sw* together and underline them with your finger. Invite him or her to identify which of the following words also begins with the *sw* initial blend: *cloud, sweep, wind*. As desired, use a similar routine for words that begin with the *sm* initial blend.

❹❺ Say the word *swans* and have the child point to the word on the chart page. Ask him or her to identify the letters *sw* and underline them with a finger. Have the child think of another word that begins with /sw/. If he or she needs assistance, sing the song together and encourage the child to identify a word in the song. As desired, use a similar routine for words beginning with /sm/.

Take-Home Phonics Story

Reading the Book in Class
- Distribute copies of pages 67–68 from the Take-Home Phonics Stories. Have children create their own books.
- For Emergent readers, read one of the books created by a child to a small group of four to six children one or more times. For Early readers, you can skip this step.
- Invite children to buddy read the book in pairs of heterogeneous stages.
- As they seem ready, have children read the book independently.

Word Bank

sw	sm
swallow	small
swans	smart
sweet	smash
sweetly	smear
swim	smell
swimming	smile
swing	smoke
swish	smooth

Connecting to Home

- Tell children to take the books they made home to share with their families once they are able to read them independently.
- Be sure to include the Parent Letter from pages 3–10 of the Take-Home Phonics Stories in the appropriate home language when you send home the book made by each child.

I found a footprint in the sand
and a big print of a hand.
I made my footprint. It was grand!
I spent the day down at the pond.

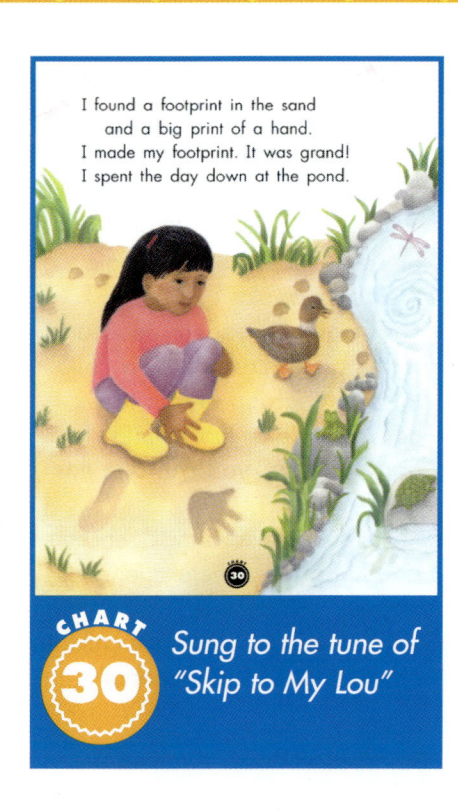

CHART 30
Sung to the tune of "Skip to My Lou"

Language Junction

Many Asian languages, including Khmer, Vietnamese, Cantonese, and Hmong, do not have consonant blends at the end of words. Children from these language backgrounds may find final blends to be a challenge. As with initial blends, some of these children may tend to introduce a short vowel sound between the consonants to make them easier to pronounce, or they may drop one of the consonant sounds.

Final Blends -nd and -nt

Setting the Scene

- Using a sand tray, make a handprint to show children what it looks like. Allow children to take turns making their own handprints. Explain to children that we can see many handprints and footprints in the sand at a beach.

Creating Comprehensible Input

- Say the chant slowly as you use gestures and pointing to make it comprehensible.

I found a footprint in the sand	point to your foot, then to the footprint on the page
and a big print of a hand.	point to your hand, then to the handprint on the page
I made my footprint. It was grand!	point to yourself, then to the footprint on the page
I spent the day down at the pond.	point to yourself, then point to the pond

Singing and Gestures

- Sing the song together as you play it on the Phonics Audio CD. Once they learn the song, teach children gestures they can make to go along with it.
- On the first line of the song, have children point to one of their feet, then to the ground, and then point to one of their hands, then to the ground.
- On the second line, invite children to take a step forward and pretend that they are making a footprint in the sand.

Recognizing Words with -nd and -nt Final Blends

- Sing the first line of the song, then point to the word *found* as you say it. Write it on the board or easel pad and say the word again. Point to the letters *nd* and tell children that the letters stand for the ending sounds they hear in *found*. Ask if they can find any other words that end like *found*. [*sand, hand, grand, pond*] Write these words under the word *found*. Tell children that there are many words that end with /nd/. Ask volunteers for any other words they can think of that end with -*nd*. Bear in mind that only children in Stages 3–5 will be able to brainstorm English words based on sounds.
- Invite children to raise their hands each time they hear /nd/ as you say the following words: *land, food, bend, pond, ball, wind, test, send, hair, mind*.
- Use a similar routine for words that end with -*nt*.

Exploring Sound-Symbol Relationships

- Use small sticky notes to cover up the first letters of each word on the chart page that ends with -*nd* or -*nt*. This will encourage children to focus on the print of -*nd* and -*nt*.
- After removing the sticky notes, invite children to come up to the chart page and practice underlining the letters that make /nd/ and /nt/ with their fingers.

STAGES ① Preproduction ② Early Production ③ Speech Emergence ④ Intermediate Fluency ⑤ Advanced Fluency

Writing Words with -nd and -nt Final Blends

- Encourage children to use their phonics skills in writing. Put away the chart page and write the following sentences on the board or easel pad:

    I made my _____.   It was _____!

- Ask volunteers to tell you what goes in the first blank. Invite the group to say the word *footprint* together, stretching the sounds.
- Ask children to tell you what letter *footprint* starts with as you write it down on the board or easel pad. Invite volunteers to come up and write the remaining letters using their phonics skills to match sounds and letters.
- Have children use their own paper to practice writing the letters in the word *footprint*.
- Use a similar procedure for the word *grand* in the blank of the second sentence.
- When you are finished, display the chart page and invite children to make comparisons between the words *footprint* and *grand* on the chart page and the same words on their own papers. Going back to the original print encourages children to use print resources in their spelling.

Using Word Wall Starters

- **Song Chart Words** Display the words *hand*, *print*, and *spent* from the Word Wall Starters pack. Ask if anyone recognizes the words. Compare the words to *hand*, *print*, and *spent* on the chart page. Invite children to tell you what letters are highlighted in yellow on each card. Use the -nd and -nt labels to start the -nd and -nt final blend sections of your Word Wall and place the cards *hand*, *print*, and *spent* beneath the appropriate labels. Later as children encounter additional -nd and -nt final blends in their reading and other class work, write each new word on an index card and highlight the final blend. Add these words to the appropriate sections of your Word Wall as well.
- **Big Book Word** After you have read the Big Book *Ibis and Jaguar's Dinner*, display the word *friend* from the Word Wall Starters pack. Using the word card and the Big Book, use a routine similar to the one above, and place the word card *friend* beneath the other words that end with -nd.

Assessment for STAGES

① ② Although these children may participate in final blend instruction, they should not be expected to master or apply it.

③ Say the word *found* and have the child point to the word on the chart page. Identify the letters -nd together and underline them with your finger. Invite him or her to identify which of the following words also ends with the -nd final blend: *band*, *like*, *cold*. As desired, use a similar routine for words that end with the -nt final blend.

④ ⑤ Say the word *found* and have the child point to the word on the chart page. Ask him or her to identify the letters -nd and underline them with a finger. Have the child think of another word that ends with /nd/. If he or she needs assistance, sing the song together and encourage the child to identify a word in the song. As desired, use a similar routine for words ending with /nt/.

Take-Home Phonics Story

Reading the Book in Class

- Distribute copies of pages 69–70 from the Take-Home Phonics Stories. Have children create their own books.
- For Emergent readers, read one of the books created by a child to a small group of four to six children one or more times. For Early readers, you can skip this step.
- Invite children to buddy read the book in pairs of heterogeneous stages.
- As they seem ready, have children read the book independently.

Word Bank

-nd	-nt
band	bent
found	cent
grand	footprint
hand	paint
kind	point
land	print
mend	rent
pond	sent
sand	spent
send	tent
wind	went

Connecting to Home

- Tell children to take the books they made home to share with their families once they are able to read them independently.
- Be sure to include the Parent Letter from pages 3–10 of the Take-Home Phonics Stories in the appropriate home language when you send home the book made by each child.

Phonics Song Chart 30   Final Blends -nd and -nt

Chart 31

Sung to the tune of "Hush, Little Baby"

First we jump and jump and jump.
Each time we jump, we make a thump!
Then we must stop and rest our feet.
We sit and rest on a swinging seat.

Extending to the -ft Final Blend

Sung to the tune of
"Hush, Little Baby"
Open the gift and look inside.
It is a raft. Let's take a ride!
Drift down the stream. Move left
 and right.
This raft is soft and very light.

Language Junction

Although there are consonant blends in Spanish, some Spanish-speaking learners of English may have difficulty with final consonant blends in English. They may tend to eliminate sounds. For example, some of these children may have a tendency to pronounce a word such as *last* as *las*.

Final Blends -st and -mp

Setting the Scene

- Bring in jump ropes for the class. Invite them to practice jumping rope.
- As children jump rope, have them listen for the sound they make each time they jump. Invite volunteers to describe the sound they make, such as *shhh* or *thump*!

Creating Comprehensible Input

- Say the chant slowly as you use gestures and pointing to make it comprehensible.

First we jump and jump and jump.	point to the girls jumping rope
Each time we jump, we make a thump!	jump up and down once
Then we must stop and rest our feet.	point to your feet
We sit and rest on a swinging seat.	point to the porch swing

Singing and Gestures

- Sing the song together as you play it on the Phonics Audio CD. Once they learn the song, teach children gestures they can make as they sing the song.
- On the first two lines, have children act out jumping rope.
- On the last two lines, have children pretend they are sitting and resting their feet.

Recognizing Words with -st and -mp Final Blends

- Sing the first line of the song, then point to the word *First* as you say it. Write it on the board or easel pad and say the word again. Point to the letters *st* and tell children that the letters stand for the ending sounds they hear in *First*. Ask if they can find any other words that end like *First*. [*must, rest*] Write these words under the word *First*. Tell children that there are many words that end with /st/. Ask volunteers for any other words they can think of that end with -st. Bear in mind that only children in Stages 3–5 will be able to brainstorm English words based on sounds.
- Invite children to pretend to rest each time they hear /st/ as you say the following words: *past, nest, laugh, just, week, list, swim, test, hand, fist*.
- Use a similar routine for words that end with -mp.

Exploring Sound-Symbol Relationships

- Use small sticky notes to cover up the last letters of each word on the chart page that ends with -st or -mp. This will encourage children to focus on the print of -st and -mp.
- After removing the sticky notes, invite children to come up to the chart page and practice underlining the letters that make /st/ and /mp/ with their fingers.

STAGES: ① Preproduction ② Early Production ③ Speech Emergence ④ Intermediate Fluency ⑤ Advanced Fluency

Writing Words with -st and -mp Final Blends

- Encourage children to use their phonics skills in writing. Put away the chart page and write the following sentence on the board or easel pad:
  _____ we jump and _____ and jump.
- Ask volunteers to tell you what goes in the first blank. Invite the group to say the word *First* together, stretching the sounds.
- Ask children to tell you what letter *First* starts with as you write it down on the board or easel pad. Invite volunteers to come up and write the remaining letters using their phonics skills to match sounds and letters.
- Have children use their own paper to practice writing the letters in the word *First*.
- Use a similar procedure for the word *jump* in the second blank in the sentence.
- When you are finished, display the chart page and invite children to make comparisons between the words *First* and *jump* on the chart page and the same words on their own papers. Going back to the original print encourages children to use print resources in their spelling.

Using Word Wall Starters

- **Song Chart Words** Display the words *rest, jump,* and *thump* from the Word Wall Starters pack. Ask if anyone recognizes the words. Compare the words to *rest, jump,* and *thump* on the chart page. Invite children to tell you what letters are highlighted in yellow on each card. Use the -st and -mp labels to start the -st and -mp final blend sections of your Word Wall and place the cards *rest, jump,* and *thump* beneath the appropriate labels. Later as children encounter additional -st and -mp final blends in their reading and other class work, write each new word on an index card and highlight the final blend. Add these words to the appropriate sections of your Word Wall as well.
- **Big Book Word** After you have read the Big Book *Ibis and Jaguar's Dinner*, display the word *must* from the Word Wall Starters pack. Using the word card and the Big Book, use a routine similar to the one above, and place the word card *must* beneath the other words that end with -st.

Assessment for STAGES

❶❷ Although these children may participate in final blend instruction, they should not be expected to master or apply it.

❸ Say the word *rest* and have the child point to the word on the chart page. Identify the letters -st together and underline them with your finger. Invite him or her to identify which of the following words also ends with the -st blend: *push, twist, fly.* As desired, use a similar routine for words that end with the -mp blend.

❹❺ Say the word *rest* and have the child point to the word on the chart page. Ask him or her to identify the letters -st and underline them with a finger. Have the child think of another word that ends with /st/. If he or she needs assistance, sing the song together and encourage the child to identify a word in the song. As desired, use a similar routine for words ending with /mp/.

Take-Home Phonics Story

Reading the Book in Class
- Distribute copies of pages 71–72 from the Take-Home Phonics Stories. Have children create their own books.
- For Emergent readers, read one of the books created by a child to a small group of four to six children one or more times. For Early readers, you can skip this step.
- Invite children to buddy read the book in pairs of heterogeneous stages.
- As they seem ready, have children read the book independently.

Word Bank

-st	-mp
best	bump
cast	camp
cost	clump
fast	damp
first	dump
just	hump
last	jump
lost	lamp
nest	lump
past	pump
rest	stump
test	thump

Connecting to Home

- Tell children to take the books they made home to share with their families once they are able to read them independently.
- Be sure to include the Parent Letter from pages 3–10 of the Take-Home Phonics Stories in the appropriate home language when you send home the book made by each child.

Phonics Song Chart 31   *Final Blends -st and -mp*

Wash, wash, wash your face.
Choose a shirt to wear.
It's time to reach for your brush.
Brush your shiny hair.

CHART 32 — *Sung to the tune of "Row, Row, Row Your Boat"*

Extending to the -nk and -ng Digraphs

Sung to the tune of "Row, Row, Row Your Boat"
Ring, ring, ring the bell.
Listen to it clank!
Ding dong, ding dong!
Give the rope a yank!

Language Junction

The sound that the digraph *sh* stands for does not exist or have a close equivalent in several languages, including Spanish, Khmer, Vietnamese, and Tagalog. Learners from those language backgrounds may have problems with producing the sound at first. Spanish-speakers may say *chip* instead of *ship*, substituting the sound that the digraph *ch* stands for.

P68

Digraphs *ch* and *sh*

Setting the Scene
- Invite children to pretend they are getting ready for school. Have them make believe they are washing their faces, brushing their hair, and choosing a shirt to wear.

Creating Comprehensible Input
- Say the chant slowly as you use gestures and pointing to make it comprehensible.

Wash, wash, wash your face.	act out washing your face
Choose a shirt to wear.	point to the shirt on the bed
It's time to reach for your brush.	point to the brush
Brush your shiny hair.	act out brushing your hair

Singing and Gestures
- Sing the song together as you play it on the Phonics Audio CD. Once they learn the song, teach children gestures they can make as they sing it again.
- Ask them to pretend they are washing their faces on the first line.
- On the second line, have them act out putting on T-shirts.
- Have children pretend they are reaching for something on the third line.
- On the last line, have children act out brushing their hair.

Recognizing Words with Digraphs *ch* and *sh*
- Sing the first line of the song, then point to the word *Wash* as you say it. Write it on the board or easel pad and say the word again. Point to the letters *sh* and tell children that these two letters stand for the ending sound they hear in *Wash*. Ask if they can find another word that ends like *Wash*. [brush] Write the word *brush* under the word *Wash*. Ask volunteers for any other words they can think of that begin and end with /sh/. Bear in mind that only children in Stages 3–5 will be able to brainstorm English words based on sounds.
- Sing the second line of the song, then point to the word *Choose* as you say it. Write it on the board or easel pad and say the word again. Point to the letters *Ch* and tell children that these two letters stand for the beginning sound they hear in *Choose*. Now ask if they can find a word that ends with /ch/. [reach] Write the word *reach* under the word *Choose*. Ask volunteers to think of other words that begin or end with /ch/.
- Invite children to pretend they are washing their faces each time they hear a word that begins or ends with /sh/: *shoe, sit, bush, pull, slip, short, push, shut, dish, shout*.
- Have children pretend to reach out in front of them as if they are reaching for a brush each time they hear a word that begins or ends with /ch/: *chip, some, chime, peach, apple, much, cherry, puppy, chimney, house*.

Exploring Sound-Symbol Relationships
- Use small sticky notes to cover up the first or last letters of words on the chart page that begin or end with *sh*. This will encourage children to focus on the print of *sh*.
- After removing the sticky notes, invite children to come up to the chart page and practice underlining the letters that make /sh/ with their fingers.
- Follow a similar routine with words that begin and end with /ch/.

STAGES ❶ Preproduction ❷ Early Production ❸ Speech Emergence ❹ Intermediate Fluency ❺ Advanced Fluency

Writing Words with Digraphs *ch* and *sh*

- Encourage children to use their phonics skills in writing. Put away the chart page and write the following sentence on the board or easel pad:
   _____ your _____ hair.
- Ask volunteers to tell you what goes in the first blank. Invite the group to say the word *Brush* together, stretching the sounds.
- Ask children to tell you what letter *Brush* starts with as you write it down on the board or easel pad. Invite volunteers to come up and write the remaining letters using their phonics skills to match sounds and letters.
- Have children use their own paper to practice writing *Brush*.
- Use a similar procedure for the word *shiny* in the second blank.
- When you are finished, display the chart page and invite children to make comparisons between the words *Brush* and *shiny* on the chart page and the same words on their own papers. Going back to the original print encourages children to use print resources in their spelling.
- Repeat the above procedure with a sentence that includes words that begin and end with /ch/.

Using Word Wall Starters

- **Song Chart Word** Display the word *reach* from the Word Wall Starters pack. Ask if anyone recognizes it. Compare the word to *reach* on the chart page. Invite children to tell you what letters are highlighted in yellow on the card. Use the *ch* label to start the *ch* digraph section of your Word Wall and place the card *reach* beneath it. Later as children encounter additional *ch* digraphs in their reading and other class work, write each new word on an index card and highlight the digraph. Add these words to this section of your Word Wall as well, grouping words with the digraph at the beginning together, and words with the digraph at the end together.
- **Big Book Word** After you have read the Big Book *Ibis and Jaguar's Dinner*, display the word *shore* from the Word Wall Starters pack. Using the word card and the Big Book, use a routine similar to the one above, and place the word card *shore* beneath the label for the *sh* digraph.

Assessment for STAGES

❶❷ Although these children may participate in digraph instruction, they should not be expected to master or apply it.

❸ Say the word *Choose* and have the child point to the word on the chart page. Identify the letters *ch* together and underline them with your finger. Invite him or her to identify which of the following words also ends with /ch/: *cup, pitch, plum*. As desired, use a similar routine for words that begin or end with the *sh* digraph.

❹❺ Say the word *Choose* and have the child point to the word on the chart page. Ask him or her to identify the letters *ch* and underline them with a finger. Have the child think of another word that ends with /ch/. If he or she needs assistance, sing the song together and encourage the child to identify a word in the song. As desired, use a similar routine for words beginning with /ch/ or beginning or ending with /sh/.

Take-Home Phonics Story

Reading the Book in Class
- Distribute copies of pages 73–74 from the Take-Home Phonics Stories. Have children create their own books.
- For Emergent readers, read one of the books created by a child to a small group of four to six children one or more times. For Early readers, you can skip this step.
- Invite children to buddy read the book in pairs of heterogeneous stages.
- As they seem ready, have children read the book independently.

Word Bank

ch	-ch	sh	-sh
chair	beach	shake	brush
chance	branch	share	cash
change	inch	shape	dish
charge	lunch	sharp	fish
chase	pinch	sheet	mash
chew	reach	shine	rash
chief	rich	shiny	rush
chin	ship	trash	
choose	shirt	wash	
chop	shop	wish	

Connecting to Home

- Tell children to take the books they made home to share with their families once they are able to read them independently.
- Be sure to include the Parent Letter from pages 3–10 of the Take-Home Phonics Stories in the appropriate home language when you send home the book made by each child.

Phonics Song Chart 32   *Digraphs ch and sh*

Chart 33
Sung to the tune of "The Wheels on the Bus"

When Keith hit a ball,
 it whirled by me
Whirled by me
Whirled by me.
When Keith hit a ball,
 it whirled by me.
I think he'll score a run!

Digraphs *th* and *wh*

Setting the Scene
- Bring in a baseball mitt and ask if anyone knows in which game it is used.
- Invite volunteers to think of other sports, such as basketball, football, and tennis and act them out. Encourage children to guess each sport.

Creating Comprehensible Input
- Say the chant slowly as you use gestures and pointing to make it comprehensible.

When Keith hit a ball, it whirled by me	point to the boy, pretend to hit a baseball, then act out trying to catch a ball
Whirled by me	act out trying to catch a ball
Whirled by me.	act out trying to catch a ball
When Keith hit a ball, it whirled by me.	point to the boy, pretend to hit a baseball, then act out trying to catch a ball
I think he'll score a run!	point to the boy, then act out cheering

Singing and Gestures
- Sing the song together as you play it on the Phonics Audio CD. Once they learn the song, teach children gestures they can make as they sing it again.
- Whenever they sing *hit a ball,* have children pretend they are hitting a baseball.
- Whenever they sing *whirled by me,* have them pretend to catch a ball.
- On the last line, ask children to pretend they are running in place, holding their hands up in the air as they cheer.

Recognizing Words with Digraphs *th* and *wh*
- Sing the first line of the song, then point to the word *When* as you say it. Write it on the board or easel pad and say the word again. Point to the letters *Wh* and tell children that these two letters stand for the beginning sound they hear in *When*. Ask if they can find another word that begins like *When*. [*whirled*] Write the word *whirled* under the word *When*. Tell children that there are many words that begin with /w/ spelled *wh*. Ask volunteers for any other words they can think of that begin with /w/ spelled *wh*.. Bear in mind that only children in Stages 3–5 will be able to brainstorm English words based on sounds.
- Sing the first line of the song again, then point to the word *Keith* as you say it. Write it on the board or easel pad and say the word again. Point to the letters *th* and tell children that these two letters stand for the ending sound they hear in *Keith*. Now ask if they can find a word that begins with /th/. [*think*] Ask volunteers to think of other words that begin or end with /th/.
- Have children pretend to catch a ball as it whirls by them each time they hear /wh/ at the beginning of words as you say the following words: *what, play, why, wheat, fall, sand, whistle, joke, sock, where*.
- Invite children to pretend to hit a ball each time they hear /th/ at the beginning or end of words as you say the following words: *thin, mix, with, thank, learn, math, jump, bath, teeth, eyes*.

Language Junction

Producing the sound that the letters *th* stand for in English may be a challenge for children from most language backgrounds. The English sounds at the beginning of *this* and *think* do not exist in many other languages, including Khmer, Cantonese, Hmong, Tagalog, Russian, and Vietnamese. Learners may substitute /t/, /d/, /z/, or other sounds for the English ones. In addition, although most Spanish speakers have a sound close to *th* with the *d* in the word *abogado,* it might be hard for them to use it at the beginning of words.

STAGES ❶ Preproduction ❷ Early Production ❸ Speech Emergence ❹ Intermediate Fluency ❺ Advanced Fluency

Exploring Sound-Symbol Relationships

- Use small sticky notes to cover up letters of each word on the chart page that begins or ends with *th*. This will encourage children to focus on the print of *th*.
- After removing the sticky notes, invite children to come up to the chart page and practice underlining the letters that make /th/.
- Follow a similar routine with words that begins with *wh*.

Writing Words with Digraphs *th* and *wh*

- Encourage children to use their phonics skills in writing. Put away the chart page and write the following sentences on the board or easel pad:
  _____ Keith hit a ball, it whirled by me.   I _____ he'll score a run!
- Ask volunteers to tell you what goes in the first blank. Invite the group to say the word *When* together, stretching the sounds.
- Ask children to tell you what letter *When* starts with as you write it down on the board or easel pad. Invite volunteers to come up and write the remaining letters.
- Have children use their own paper to practice writing *When*.
- Use a similar procedure for the word *think* in the second sentence.
- Display the chart page and invite children to make comparisons between the words *When* and *think* on the chart page and the same words on their own papers.

Using Word Wall Starters

- **Song Chart Words** Display the words *Keith*, *think*, and *when* from the Word Wall Starters pack. Compare the words to *Keith*, *think*, and *When* on the chart page. Invite children to tell you what letters are highlighted in yellow on each card. Use the *th* and *wh* labels to start the *th* and *wh* digraph sections of your Word Wall and place the cards *Keith*, *think*, and *when* beneath the appropriate labels. As children encounter additional *th* and *wh* digraphs in their class work, write each new word on an index card, highlight the digraph, and add these words to your Word Wall.
- **Big Book Word** After you have read the Big Book *Ibis and Jaguar's Dinner*, display the word *what* from the Word Wall Starters pack. Using the word card and the Big Book, use a routine similar to the one above, and place the word card *what* beneath the label for the *wh* digraph.

Assessment for STAGES

❶❷ Although these children may participate in digraph instruction, they should not be expected to master or apply it.

❸ Say the word *Keith* and have the child point to the word on the chart page. Identify the letters *th* together and underline them with your finger. Invite the child to identify which of the following words also ends with /th/: *fourth*, *make*, *dirt*. As desired, use a similar routine for words that begin with the initial digraph *wh*.

❹❺ Say the word *Keith* and have the child point to the word on the chart page. Ask him or her to identify the letters *th* and underline them with a finger. Have the child think of another word that ends with /th/. If he or she needs assistance, sing the song together and encourage the child to identify a word in the song. As desired, use a similar routine for words beginning with /th/ and /w/.

Take-Home Phonics Story

Reading the Book in Class

- Distribute copies of pages 75–76 from the Take-Home Phonics Stories. Have children create their own books.
- For Emergent readers, read one of the books created by a child to a small group of four to six children one or more times. For Early readers, you can skip this step.
- Invite children to buddy read the book in pairs of heterogeneous stages.
- As they seem ready, have children read the book independently.

Word Bank

th	-th	wh
thank	bath	whale
thick	Beth	what
thin	booth	wheel
thing	broth	when
think	cloth	where
third	Keith	which
thirsty	math	while
thirty	path	whirled
those	tooth	white
Thursday	truth	why

Connecting to Home

- Tell children to take the books they made home to share with their families once they are able to read them independently.
- Be sure to include the Parent Letter from pages 3–10 of the Take-Home Phonics Stories in the appropriate home language when you send home the book made by each child.

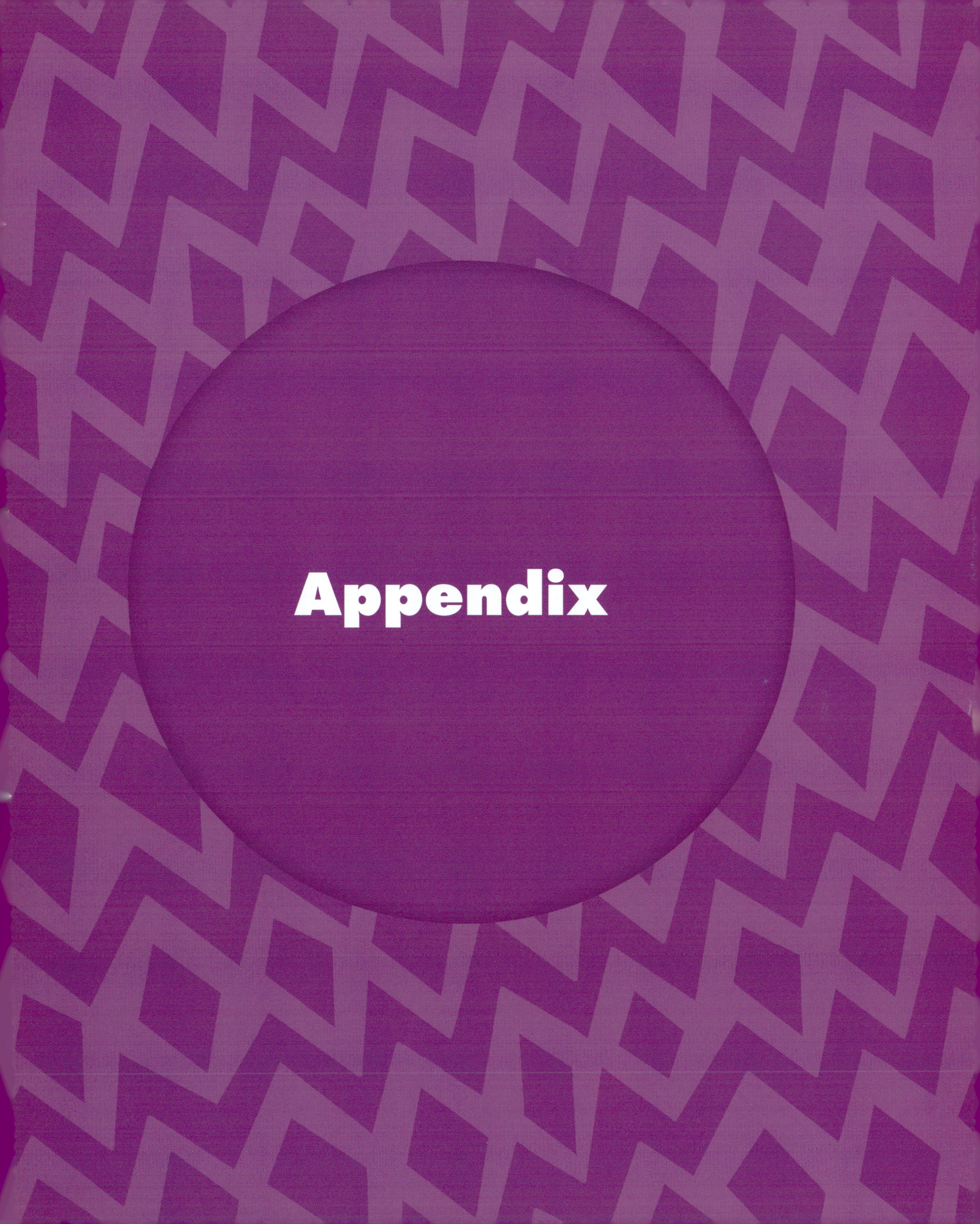

Appendix

Appendix

Oral Language Rubric A2

Letter Recognition Record A3

Letter Formation Record A4

K–5 Scope and Sequence A5

Language Functions Scope A13

Language Learning Strategies Scope A14

Bibliography A16

Oral Language Rubric for *On Our Way to English*

STAGE 1: Preproduction	**Comprehension** Understands little of everyday English. **Message** Communicates primarily through gestures or single-word utterances. Able to communicate only the most rudimentary needs. **Fluency and Sentence Structure** Produces little, if any, spoken English.
STAGE 2: Early Production	**Comprehension** Understands some social conversation but limited academic conversation. **Message** Uses routine expressions to convey basic needs and ideas. To some extent, continues to rely on gestures to communicate. **Fluency and Sentence Structure** Uses some basic words and simple phrases. **Word Choice and Academic Language** Relies on routine language expressions. May use some academic words in isolation.
STAGE 3: Speech Emergence	**Comprehension** Understands most of what is said in social and academic conversation but exhibits occasional lack of understanding. **Message** Participates in everyday conversations about familiar topics. Although speech contains errors that sometimes hinder communication, child can often convey his or her basic message. **Fluency and Sentence Structure** Produces longer, complete phrases and some sentences. **Word Choice and Academic Language** Relies on high-frequency words and sometimes cannot fully communicate ideas due to a lack of sufficient vocabulary. Uses some academic language although not always successfully.
STAGE 4: Intermediate Fluency	**Comprehension** Rarely experiences a lack of understanding in social and academic situations. **Message** Engages in ordinary conversation. Although errors may be present, they generally do not hinder communication. Successfully communicates most ideas to others. **Fluency and Sentence Structure** Engages in ordinary conversation with some complex sentences. Errors no longer hinder communication. **Word Choice and Academic Language** Range of vocabulary and academic language allows child to communicate well on everyday topics. Begins to use idioms. Occasionally uses inappropriate terms and/or must rephrase to work around unknown vocabulary.
STAGE 5: Advanced Fluency	**Comprehension** Understands social and academic conversation without difficulty. **Message** Uses English successfully to convey his or her ideas to others. **Fluency and Sentence Structure** Speech appears to be fluent and effortless, approximating that of native-speaking peers. **Word Choice and Academic Language** Use of vocabulary, academic language, and idioms approximates that of native-speaking peers.

Letter Recognition Record

Name: _____
Grade: _____
Age: _____
Date: _____

Point to a letter and say, "Tell me what this is." Mark as indicated below.

  ✓ = correct response (letter name, word, or sound)
  ✗ = incorrect response
  O = no response

G	T	M	L	Q	C	J
U	V	B	R	W	O	E
D	F	Z	S	H	X	N
K	A	Y	P	I		
g	t	m	l	q	c	j
u	v	b	r	w	o	e
d	f	z	s	h	x	n
k	a	y	p	i		

Total correct: _____
Comments: _____
_____
_____

© 2004 Rigby

Letter Recognition Record *On Our Way to English*

Letter Formation Record

Name: _____

Grade: _____

Age: _____

Date: _____

Have the child write the lowercase alphabet and the uppercase alphabet on a sheet of paper. Use this form to indicate which letters are written accurately (checkmark) and which ones need further practice (circle).

Key: __✓__ = formed correctly

__O__ = needs further practice

a	b	c	d	e	f	g
h	i	j	k	l	m	n
o	p	q	r	s	t	u
v	w	x	y	z		
A	B	C	D	E	F	G
H	I	J	K	L	M	N
O	P	Q	R	S	T	U
V	W	X	Y	Z		

© 2004 Rigby

A4   Letter Formation Record

K–5 Scope and Sequence

Comprehension

	K	1	2	3	4	5
Uses prior knowledge and experiences						
Activates existing background knowledge	●	●	●	●		
Makes connections with text based on personal experiences and knowledge					●	●
Makes connections with text based on educational experience and knowledge					●	●
Builds background knowledge	●	●	●	●		
Uses illustrations and text features to help store important new information					●	●
Determines what is important in text						
Recognizes how readers use capitalization and punctuation to comprehend	●					
Identifies main ideas or theme	●	●	●	●		
Identifies main ideas and supporting details					●	●
Utilizes text features and text structures to determine importance			●	●		
Uses personal beliefs, experiences, and prior learning to determine importance					●	●
Recognizes cause and effect			●	●	●	●
Compares and contrasts information	●	●	●	●		
Classifies and ranks important vs. unimportant information					●	●
Considers purpose for reading	●	●	●	●	●	●
Recognizes theme and relevance to reader						●
Draws inferences						
Makes and confirms predictions	●	●	●	●		
Makes, changes, and checks predictions					●	●
Draws conclusions with support drawn from text		●	●	●	●	●
Makes generalizations			●	●	●	●
Forms and supports opinions			●	●		
Creates personal interpretations			●	●		
Forms personal interpretations					●	●
Makes critical judgments					●	●
Asks questions						
Asks questions to clarify meaning	●	●	●	●		
Asks in order to clarify and extend comprehension					●	●
Asks questions to understand author		●	●	●		
Asks questions to understand key themes		●	●	●		
Asks in order to preview, plan reading, and predict					●	●
Asks in order to understand how genre influences comprehension					●	●
Asks to recognize and interpret story elements and text features				●	●	●

K–5 Scope and Sequence   On Our Way to English   A5

	K	1	2	3	4	5
Synthesizes Information						
Connects ideas from several different sources 　　Text-to-text 　　Text-to-self 　　Text-to-world		●	●	●	●	●
Sequences ideas and story events	●	●	●	●	●	●
Summarizes information		●	●	●	●	●
Classifies and categorizes information	●	●	●	●		
Retells story events or key facts	●	●	●	●		
Retells in order to clarify					●	●
Considers author's viewpoint, purpose, and style			●	●	●	●
Focuses on text elements to understand overall meaning and theme					●	●
Shares, recommends, and criticizes what is read				●	●	●
Reacts to and interprets what is read				●	●	●
Uses sensory images						
Creates or uses images from all senses	●	●	●	●		
Makes connections with all 5 senses and with emotions					●	●
Visualizes information from text, illustrations, diagrams, etc.	●	●	●	●	●	●
Uses fix-up strategies to monitor comprehension						
Rereads text	●	●	●	●		
Rereads and reviews text					●	●
Reads on		●	●	●	●	●
Adjusts pace			●	●	●	●
Uses decoding skills	●	●	●	●		
Uses decoding, word analysis, syntactic and context clues for word recognition or pronunciation					●	●
Self-monitors by asking questions		●	●	●		
Changes mind while reading						●
Identifies synonyms, antonyms, homonyms, homophones				●	●	●

Literacy Skills

Phonological Awareness

	K	1	2	3	4	5
Identifies words within sentences *(see also Concepts of Print)*	●	●				
Identifies syllables within spoken words	●	●				
Recognizes and produces rhyming words	●	●	●	●		
Identifies and isolates initial and final sounds in spoken words	●	●	●			
Identifies and matches initial and final sounds in spoken words	●	●	●			
Blends phonemes to make words	●	●	●			
Segments one-syllable words into initial, medial, and final sounds	●	●	●			
Deletes phonemes to change words		●	●			
Adds phonemes to change words		●	●			

A6

	K	1	2	3	4	5

Phonics and decoding

	K	1	2	3	4	5
Names and identifies letters of the alphabet	●	●				
Knows order of the alphabet	●	●				
Uses knowledge of letter-sound relationships to decode	●	●	●	●	●	●
Develops and applies knowledge of consonant sounds		●	●	●	●	●
Develops and applies knowledge of consonant blends		●	●	●	●	●
Develops and applies knowledge of consonant digraphs		●	●	●	●	●
Develops and applies knowledge of consonant patterns, such as *kn, wr, dge, tch*				●	●	●
Develops and applies knowledge of short vowels	●	●	●	●	●	●
Develops and applies knowledge of long vowels		●	●	●	●	●
Develops and applies knowledge of complex vowel patterns: *oo, au, aw, al, all*			●	●	●	●
Uses knowledge of vowel diphthongs		●	●	●	●	●
Uses knowledge of vowel digraphs		●	●	●	●	●
Uses knowledge of vowel variants, i.e. one vowel sound can have more than one spelling (e.g., *clue, new, to*) or one spelling can have more than one sound		●	●	●	●	●
Demonstrates understanding of *r*-controlled vowels		●	●	●	●	●
Uses knowledge of word families to decode		●	●	●	●	●
Reads more complex and irregularly spelled words		●	●	●	●	●
Uses knowledge of spelling patterns to decode (CVC, CVCe, CV)		●	●	●	●	●
Uses knowledge of syllables to decode multi-syllable words		●	●	●	●	●

Concepts of Print and Structural Analysis

	K	1	2	3	4	5
Develops an understanding of letters and words	●	●				
Develops an understanding of sentences and paragraphs		●	●	●		
Understands that a sentence begins with a capital letter	●	●	●			
Uses knowledge of word order and context to support word identification and confirm word meaning [e.g., Child uses decoding skills and predicts meaning, then sees if predicted meaning makes sense given the position of the word in the sentence (subject, verb, object) and given the context.]		●	●	●	●	●
Demonstrates book-handling skills	●	●	●	●	●	●
Demonstrates directionality	●	●	●	●	●	●
Identifies uppercase and lowercase letters	●	●	●		●	
Understands words are separated by spaces	●	●	●	●	●	●
Matches spoken words to print	●	●	●	●	●	●
Recognizes parts of a book (cover, title, title page)	●	●	●	●	●	●
Recognizes name and common environmental print	●	●	●	●	●	●
Locates name of author and illustrator	●	●	●	●	●	●
Identifies end punctuation	●	●	●	●	●	●
Reads one-syllable and high-frequency words	●	●	●	●	●	●

K–5 Scope and Sequence   *On Our Way to English*   A7

	K	1	2	3	4	5
Concepts of Print and Structural Analysis *(continued)*						
Demonstrates understanding of how type treatment can convey meaning (e.g., boldface, italics, falling or slanted letters, reverse out of color)		●	●	●		
Uses picture cues to comprehend text	●	●	●	●	●	●
Demonstrates understanding of inflected endings *(-ed, -ing, -s)*	●	●	●	●	●	●
Demonstrates an understanding of noun plurals	●	●	●	●	●	●
Identifies and reads compound words		●	●	●	●	●
Identifies and reads contractions		●	●	●	●	●
Demonstrates understanding of possessives	●	●	●	●	●	●
Uses knowledge of prefixes and suffixes			●	●	●	●
Identifies root words		●		●	●	●
Literary Response/Analysis						
Distinguishes genres (e.g., play, fiction, nonfiction, poetry, fable or fairy tale, traditional tale, drama, letter, e-mail)		●	●	●	●	●
Distinguishes fantasy from reality	●	●	●	●	●	●
Distinguishes fact from opinion			●	●	●	●
Understands role of author and illustrator		●	●	●	●	●
Understands characters and setting	●	●	●	●	●	●
Identifies sequence of events, problem, and solution		●	●		●	
Identifies plot (story problem), conflict, and sequence of events				●		●
Identifies beginning, middle, end	●	●	●	●	●	
Recognizes table of contents and chapter titles				●	●	●
Recognizes point of view				●	●	●
Identifies mood				●	●	●
Compares and contrasts plots (story problem), settings, and characters		●	●	●	●	●
Compares and contrasts different forms of the same story			●	●	●	●
Identifies author's style of writing					●	●
Understands use of dialogue in text	●	●	●	●	●	●
Understands use of dialogue in play		●	●	●	●	●
Recognizes descriptive language and imagery			●	●	●	●
Identifies rhythm, rhyme, and alliteration	●	●	●	●	●	●
Identifies onomatopoeia		●	●	●	●	●
Identifies and understands use of figurative language			●	●	●	●
Identifies and understands use of personification			●	●	●	●
Identifies and understands use of metaphor				●	●	●
Identifies and understands use of simile				●	●	●
Recognizes humor in text	●	●	●	●	●	●
Recognizes use of exaggeration in text				●	●	●
Identifies use of flashbacks				●	●	●
Identifies use of foreshadowing				●		●

A8

	K	1	2	3	4	5
Literary Response/Analysis *(continued)*						
Recognizes idioms	●	●	●	●	●	●
Recognizes use of suspense					●	●
Discusses a range of books and stories	●	●	●	●	●	●
Takes notes on nonfiction reading				●	●	●
Uses graphic organizers to organize information				●	●	●

Nonfiction

Text features

	K	1	2	3	4	5
Recognizes and uses contents page	●	●	●	●	●	●
Recognizes and uses picture index	●	●				
Recognizes and uses index			●	●	●	●
Uses alphabet knowledge to locate information		●	●	●	●	●
Uses glossary		●	●	●	●	●
Recognizes headings and subheadings		●	●	●	●	●
Uses photos and illustrations	●	●	●	●	●	●
Reads labels	●	●	●	●	●	●
Reads captions			●	●	●	●
Uses recipe			●	●	●	●
Uses lists and bullet points		●	●	●	●	●
Uses inserted information		●	●	●	●	●
Uses sidebars and boxes				●	●	●
Uses guide words	●	●	●	●	●	●

Graphic elements

	K	1	2	3	4	5
Uses maps			●	●	●	●
Uses charts and diagrams	●	●	●	●	●	●
Uses cross sections and cutaways				●	●	●
Uses bird's eye view			●	●	●	●
Uses graphs				●	●	●
Uses time lines			●	●	●	●
Uses scale drawings				●	●	●
Uses floor plans				●	●	●
Uses flow charts					●	●
Uses satellite or radar images				●	●	●
Uses microscopic images						●

Types of nonfiction

	K	1	2	3	4	5
Understands and uses question & answer format		●	●	●	●	●
Understands reference			●	●	●	●
Understands how-to instructions		●	●	●	●	●
Recognizes journals/observation logs			●	●	●	●

	K	1	2	3	4	5
Types of nonfiction *(continued)*						
Understands explanation		●	●	●	●	●
Understands narrative account	●	●	●	●	●	●
Recognizes description			●	●	●	●
Understands photo essay				●	●	●
Recognizes persuasive language			●	●	●	●
Recognizes compare/contrast				●	●	●
Understands interview			●	●	●	●
Understands biography			●	●	●	●
Grammar						
Adjectives	●	●	●	●	●	●
Adverbs	●	●	●	●	●	●
Conjunctions	●	●	●	●	●	●
Interjections					●	●
Prepositions	●	●	●	●	●	●
Pronouns	●	●	●	●	●	●
Nouns	●	●	●	●	●	●
Verbs						
Future Tense	●	●	●	●	●	●
Past Tense		●	●	●	●	●
Present Tense	●	●	●	●	●	●
Continuous	●	●	●	●	●	●
Perfect			●	●	●	●
Passive			●	●	●	●
Helping Verbs			●	●	●	●
Linking Verbs	●	●	●	●	●	●
Gerunds				●	●	●
Infinitives	●	●	●	●	●	●
Commands	●	●	●	●	●	●
Exclamations	●	●	●	●	●	●
Statements	●	●	●	●	●	●
Questions	●	●	●	●	●	●
Negative Sentences	●	●	●	●	●	●
Complex Sentences		●	●	●	●	●
Compound Sentences		●	●	●	●	●
Compound-Complex Sentences				●	●	●
Comparative and Superlative	●	●	●	●	●	●
Contractions		●	●	●	●	●
Possessives	●	●	●	●	●	●

A10

Writing

	K	1	2	3	4	5
Strategies						
Participates in collaborative writing, shared writing, and writing to prompts	●	●	●	●	●	●
Uses a variety of prewriting strategies [drawing, graphic organizers, brainstorming, notes]	●	●	●	●	●	●
Writing process: prewriting, writing drafts, revising, proofreading, publishing		●	●	●	●	●
Evaluates own writing and peers' writing						
Applications						
Writes sentences	●	●	●	●	●	●
Writes labels, captions, lists, logs	●	●	●	●	●	●
Writes to retell personal experiences [dictation, language experience]	●	●	●			
Writes narrative text based on personal experience			●	●	●	●
Writes narrative text [humorous, realistic, fantasy]				●	●	●
Writes to entertain [stories, poems]				●	●	●
Writes letters [informal, formal]				●	●	●
Writes expository text [reports, instructions, steps in a process, research results, comparison-contrast, cause-effect]		●	●	●	●	●
Writes persuasive text [review, letter, request]				●	●	●
Writes using point of view					●	●
Organization and Focus						
Uses models and traditional structures for writing		●	●	●	●	●
Writes to communicate ideas and reflections		●	●	●	●	●
Maintains a central idea or single focus		●	●	●	●	●
Presents information in a logical sequence			●	●	●	●
Addresses purposes and audience		●	●	●	●	●
Addresses length and format					●	●
Uses descriptive words		●	●	●	●	●
Uses dialogue					●	●
Uses topic sentences with supporting sentences in writing		●	●	●	●	●
Writes with a distinct beginning, middle, and end				●	●	●
Uses paragraphs effectively in writing				●	●	●

K–5 Scope and Sequence   On Our Way to English   A11

	K	1	2	3	4	5
Evaluation and Revision						
Revises to improve progression and clarity of ideas				●	●	●
Revises to include more descriptive and sensory detail			●	●	●	●
Adds titles and headings			●	●	●	●
Revises to vary sentence structure			●	●	●	●
Combines sentences		●	●	●	●	●
Revises to improve word choice		●	●	●	●	●
Proofreads to correct spelling				●	●	●
Uses a variety of reference materials to revise [dictionary, thesaurus, Internet, proofreading checklist]				●	●	●
Comments constructively on peers' writing and revises based on peer comments		●	●	●	●	●
Uses proofreading symbols to revise		●	●	●	●	●
Sentence Structure and Grammar						
Uses complete sentences and recognizes correct word order			●	●	●	●
Uses simple and complex sentences		●	●	●	●	●
Demonstrates an understanding of subject-verb agreement		●	●	●	●	●
Uses appropriate parts of speech			●	●	●	●
Uses basic capitalization and punctuation rules		●	●	●	●	●
Penmanship						
Writes uppercase and lowercase letters of the alphabet	●	●	●	●	●	●
Writes clearly and legibly		●	●	●	●	●
Allows adequate spacing between letters, words, and sentences	●	●	●	●	●	●
Punctuation						
Uses end punctuation	●	●	●	●	●	●
Uses commas			●	●	●	●
Uses quotation marks				●	●	●
Uses apostrophes in possessive nouns and in contractions			●	●	●	●

Language Functions Scope

Social Function	Definition	Stages of Oral Language Development (1-5)	K-5
Agree and disagree	express opinion regarding ideas, actions, etc.	1,2,3,4,5	K,1,2,3
Apologize	express remorse for an action or something said	1,2,3,4,5	K,3
Ask for assistance or permission	use question words to make requests or ask for clarification; request permission; make requests	2,3,4,5	K,1,3,4,5
Express feelings and needs	use words to express emotions, ideas and feelings, refuse	1,2,3,4,5	K,1,3,4,5
Express likes and dislikes	use words to express likes/dislikes and preferences; express opinions about film, print, and technological presentations with supporting examples	1,2,3,4,5	K,1,2,4,5
Express obligation	indicate that something should be done to benefit oneself or others, for example, We should take care of our planet.	3,4,5	1,2,4,5
Give instructions	inform or direct a person by telling, explaining, or describing	2,3,4,5	3,4,5
Greet	use appropriate phrases for welcoming someone, greeting, making introductions, making small talk such as How are you? What's new?; saying and responding to farewell	1,2,3,4,5	K,1,2,3
Negotiate	propose ways of proceeding in group work that recognize the need for compromise and diplomacy	3,4,5	3,4,5
Use appropriate register	vary degree of formality in speech (word choice, diction, and usage) according to setting, occasion, purpose, and audience	3,4,5	3,4,5
Use social etiquette	respond appropriately and courteously to directions and questions; express gratitude; appropriately use polite phrases such as please, thank you, excuse me	1,2,3,4,5	K,1,2,3
Warn	inform of danger; command that someone should or should not do something for safety	1,2,3,4,5	K,2,5
Wish and hope	use words to express a desire such as I hope I can go to the game; I wish it would snow.	3,4,5	1,2,4

Academic Function	Definition	Stages of Oral Language Development	K-5
Analyze	separate whole into parts; identify relationships and patterns; identify cause and effect; interpret important events and ideas	3,4,5	1,2,3,4,5
Classify	group objects or ideas according to their characteristics	1,2,3,4,5	K,3
Compare (and contrast)	describe similarity and/or differences in objects or ideas or between print, visual, and electronic media	2,3,4,5	K,1,2,4,5
Describe	name; describe immediate surroundings; give and account of an event/action, object, person, and/or characteristics in words	2,3,4,5	K,1,4,5
Evaluate	assess and verify the worth of an object, idea or decision	3,4,5	2,3
Explain	express an understanding of a process, an event, or idea (gleaned from video segments, graphic art, or technology presentations); give the "why" when providing information; ask questions to obtain information or directions	3,4,5	1,3,5
Express position	tell where something is (here, there, right/left, up/down); use prepositional phrases of location	2,3,4,5	K,1
Inquire	ask questions to obtain information or directions	2,3,4,5	K,1,2
Justify and persuade	give reasons for an action, decision, point of view; convince others by clarifying and supporting with evidence, elaborations, and examples	3,4,5	2,4,5
Predict and hypothesize	suggest cause or outcomes	1,2,3,4,5	K,2,3,5
Report	share or recount personal or other factual information	3,4,5	1,3
Sequence	put objects, ideas, numbers, or events into a particular order through retelling, role-playing, and/or visually illustrating	1,2,3,4,5	K,2,4
Solve problems	define and represent a problem and determine a solution	3,4,5	3,5
Synthesize	combine or integrate spoken ideas to form a new whole; summarize orally; draw conclusions from information gathered from multiple sources	3,4,5	3,4,5
Tell time	use words and expressions to express hours and time; talk about calendar	1,2,3,4,5	K,1,4

Language Functions Scope   On Our Way to English   A13

Language Learning Strategies Scope

Student Language	Teacher Language	Definitions and/or Examples	1 2 3 4 5 STAGES OF ORAL LANGUAGE DEVELOPMENT	K 1 2 3 4 5
• Ask for help in your home language.	• Use home language for clarification.	• Student talks to someone in his or her home language to find out the meaning of an unknown word or phrase.	● ● ● ● ●	● ●
• Show me what you mean.	• Manipulate and act out language.	• Student uses real objects and role-playing to communicate.	● ● ● ● ●	●
• Ask or show me when you need help.	• Ask for adult assistance.	• Student requests help from an adult (verbally and nonverbally).	● ● ● ● ●	●
• Look at what I do when I talk.	• Compare verbal and nonverbal cues.	• Ex: Teacher says, "Smile." Student is confused until seeing the teacher point to his/her mouth, then student performs the action.	● ● ● ● ●	●
• When you talk to adults, call them Mr., Ms., or Mrs. with their last name. • Use different kinds of words in different settings.	• Rehearse variations of language in different social and academic settings.	• Ex: Student calls friends by their first names, but knows to address teachers with titles such as Mr. and Mrs. • Ex: Student learns the difference between using the term *soil* in the classroom and *dirt* when playing.	● ● ● ●	● ●
• Practice what you learn.	• Test new expressions through use.	• Student learns new word or phrase and practices using it.	● ● ● ● ●	● ●
• Say what another child says.	• Imitate others' language use.	• Ex: Student hears a classmate use the word *please* or *it's your turn* and imitates.	● ● ● ● ●	●
• Put new words in sentences you know. • Use language you know.	• Learn to use language patterns.	• Student identifies and correctly uses a phrase or sentence pattern. Ex: *We have _____.* • Student identifies and correctly uses a phrase or sentence pattern. Ex: *I got five* when sharing answers to a math problem	● ● ● ●	● ● ● ●
• Ask or show me when you don't understand. • Ask me "What do you mean?" when you don't understand.	• Seek clarification.	• Student uses gesture, word, or phrase to ask for clarification. Ex: *What do you mean? What is _____?*	● ● ● ●	● ●
• Try saying that again another way.	• Clarify and restate information.	• Students restate what they have said when communication breaks down.	● ● ●	●
• Tell a friend how to say that. • Teach a friend.	• Teach a peer.	• Student practices recently learned vocabulary, phrases, and expressions by teaching a peer.	● ● ● ●	● ●
• Talk around the problem word.	• Paraphrase.	• Student "talks around" an unknown word, hoping to get the meaning across. Ex: *The things that you use to put flowers in.* (vase)	● ● ● ●	● ● ● ● ●
• Ask "Do you understand?" • Ask "Did I say that right?"	• Seek feedback. • Get feedback.	• Ex: Students seek feedback on language use.	● ● ●	● ● ● ●
• Try a word and see if it works.	• Coin a word.	• Student makes up a word to describe something, hoping that someone will supply the target word. Ex: *bee house* (bee hive)	● ● ●	● ●

A14

Student Language	Teacher Language	Definitions and/or Examples	1 2 3 4 5 STAGES OF ORAL LANGUAGE DEVELOPMENT	K 1 2 3 4 5
• Use your home language to help you understand a word. • How can your home language help you?	• Use a cognate.	• Student uses a home language word, hoping that it is similar to a word in the target language. Ex: *I went to the parque.* (park) • Student uses the meaning of a similar word in the home language to understand English.	● ● ● ● ●	● ● ●
• Listen for parts you know. • Listen for important parts.	• Attend selectively to input.	• Student focuses on breaking down a sentence into understandable language patterns or "chunks." Ex: Teacher says "We're going to do some writing. Take out your paper and pencil." Student focuses on materials needed, i.e., words *paper* and *pencil*. • Student learns to listen for key ideas and details.	● ● ● ●	● ●
• Work with a friend to help you understand. • Ask a friend for help.	• Consult a peer.	• Student talks to a classmate to develop understanding. • Student asks peers, both English language learners and native English speakers, for help.	● ● ● ● ●	● ●
• It's OK to use things written in your home language to help you. • Look in a book in your home language for help.	• Consult home language resources.	• Student uses written home language resources, such as books, picture cards, or dictionary.	● ● ● ● ●	● ●
• Sometimes you don't need to know the meaning of every single word to understand. • Keep listening when you don't understand a word.	• Skip an unknown word as necessary.	• Student skims over unknown words in order to focus on the full meaning of a phrase, sentence, or paragraph. Ex: *The spotted dog played in the street* can be mostly understood without the word *spotted*. • If students keep listening, they may find that they didn't need to understand a particular word or that context may help them understand it.	● ● ●	● ●
• Keep using words you've learned in our theme.	• Use academic language across content areas.	• Student uses academic language learned, such as *equal, compare,* and *soil*.	● ● ● ● ●	● ● ●
• Write down what you learn to help you remember.	• Take notes to help you remember.	• Student learns to write down key ideas and details in note form.	● ● ● ●	● ●

Language Learning Strategies Scope — *On Our Way to English*

Bibliography

Adams, Marilyn J. *Beginning to Read: Thinking and Learning About Print.* Cambridge: MIT Press, 1990.

Adams, M., Foorman, B., I. Lundberg, and T. Beeler. *Phonemic Awareness in Young Children.* Baltimore: Paul Brookes, 1998.

Allen, V. *Selecting Materials for the Reading Instructions of ESL Children. Kids Come in All Languages: Reading Instructions for ESL Students,* edited by K. Spandenburg-Urbschat and R. Pritchard. Newark: International Reading Association, 1994.

Amador-Watson, C. *Introduction to Guided Reading for Emergent and Early Readers Seminar.* Crystal Lake, IL: Rigby, 1999.

Amador-Watson, Clara and Charlotte Knox. *Responsive Instruction for Success in English.* Crystal Lake, IL: Rigby, 2000.

Anderson, Neil. *Exploring Second Language Reading: Issues and Strategies.* Boston: Heinle & Heinle, 1999.

Au, Kathryn H. *Literacy Instruction in Multicultural Settings.* New York: Harcourt Brace, 1993.

August, D., and K. Hakuta, eds. *Improving Schooling for Language Minority Children: A Research Agenda.* National Research Council. Washington, DC: National Academy Press, 1997.

Baker, Colin. *Foundations of Bilingual Education and Bilingualism.* 2d ed. Bristol, PA: Multilingual Matters, 1996.

Bear, Donald R., et al. *Words Their Way: Word Study for Phonics, Vocabulary, and Spelling Instruction.* Upper Saddle River, NJ: Merrill, 1999.

Bisplinghoff, B. and J. Allen. *Engaging Teachers: Creative Teaching and Researching Relationships.* York, ME: Stenhouse, 1998.

Boyle, O. and S. Peregoy. "Literacy Scaffolds: Strategies for First- and Second-Language Readers and Writers." *The Reading Teacher,* 1990.

Bransford, J. and D. L. Swartz. "Rethinking Transfer: A Simple Proposal with Multiple Implications." In *Review of Educational Research: Volume 24,* edited by A. Iran-Nejad and P. D. Pearson. Washington, DC: American Educational Research Association, 1999.

Brantley, Jane H. *Basically Phonics Facilitator's Manual.* Crystal Lake, IL: Rigby, 1998.

Brisk, María Estela, and Margaret M. Harrington. *Literacy and Bilingualism: A Handbook for All Teachers.* Mahwah, NJ: Lawrence Erlbaum Associates, 2000.

Brown, H. Douglas. *Teaching by Principles: An Interactive Approach to Language Pedagogy.* Englewood Cliffs, NJ: Prentice Hall Regents, 1994.

Brown, James Dean. *The Elements of Language Curriculum: A Systematic Approach to Program Development.* Boston: Heinle & Heinle, 1995.

Cambourne, B., and J. Turbill. *Responsive Evaluation: Making Valid Judgments About Student Literacy.* Portsmouth, NH: Heinemann, 1994.

Campbell, Cherry. *Teaching Second-Language Writing: Interacting with Text.* Boston: Heinle & Heinle, 1998.

Cary, Stephen. *Second Language Learners.* York, ME: Stenhouse Publishers, 1997.

Celce-Murcia, Marianne, ed. *Teaching English as a Second or Foreign Language.* 2d ed. Boston: Heinle & Heinle, 1991.

Chamot, Anna Uhl, et al. *The CALLA Handbook: Implementing the Cognitive Academic Language Learning Approach.* Reading, MA: Addison-Wesley, 1994.

Chamot, Anna Uhl, Sarah Barnhardt, Pamela Bread El-Dinary, and Jill Robins. *The Learning Strategies Handbook.* White Plains, NY: Longman, 1999.

Chard, David J., and Shirley V. Dickson. "Phonological Awareness: Instructional and Assessment Guidelines." *Intervention in School and Clinic:* Vol. 34, No. 5, 1999.

Clark, Raymond C., Patrick R. Moran, and Arthur A. Burrows. *The ESL Miscellany.* Brattleboro, VT: Pro Lingua Associates, 1991.

Clay, Marie M. *Becoming Literate: The Construction of Inner Control.* Portsmouth, NH: Heinemann, 1991.

———. *Reading Recovery: A Guidebook for Teachers in Training.* Portsmouth, NH: Heinemann, 1993.

———. *An Observation Survey of Early Literacy Achievement.* Portsmouth, NH: Heinemann, 1993.

———. *Becoming Literate: The Construction of Inner Control.* Portsmouth, NH: Heinemann, 1997.

———. *By Different Paths to Common Outcomes.* York, Maine: Stenhouse, 1998.

Cloud, Nancy, Fred Genesee, and Else Hamayan. *Dual Language Instruction: A Handbook for Enriched Education.* Boston: Heinle & Heinle, 2000.

Coles, Gerald. *Misreading Reading: The Bad Science That Hurts Children.* Portsmouth, NH: Heinemann, 2000.

Collier, V. "How Long? A Synthesis of Research on Academic Achievement in a Second Language." *TESOL Quarterly* 23(3), 509–532, 1989.

Collier, V. P. *Promoting Academic Success for ESL Students.* Jersey City: New Jersey Teachers of English to Speakers of Other Languages–Bilingual Educators, 1995.

Collins, A., J. Brown, and S. Newman. "Cognitive Apprenticeship: Teaching the Crafts of Reading, Writing, and Mathematics." In *Knowing, Learning, and Instructions: Essays in Honor of Robert Glaser,* edited by L. Resnick. Hillsdale, NJ: Lawrence Erlbaum Associates, 1989.

Crystal, D. *A Dictionary of Linguistics and Phonetics.* Cambridge: Basil Blackwell, 1980.

Cummins, J. *Negotiating Identities: Education for Empowerment in a Diverse Society.* Ontario, CA: California Association for Bilingual Education, 1996.

———. *Language, Power and Pedagogy: Bilingual Children in the Crossfire.* Tonawnada, NY: Multilingual Matters, 2000.

———. *Negotiating Identities: Education for Empowerment in a Diverse Society.* Ontario, CA: California Association for Bilingual Education, 1996.

———. "The Acquisition of English as a Second Language." In *Kids Come in All Languages: Reading for Instruction for ESL Students.* Newark, DE: International Reading Association, 1994.

———. *Empowering Minority Students.* Sacramento: CABE, 1989.

———. "Age on Arrival and Immigrant Second Language Learning in Canada: A Reassessment." *Applied Linguistics* 2, 132–149, 1981.

———. "The Role of Primary Language Development in Promoting Educational Success for Language Minority Students." In *Schooling and Language Minority Students: A Theoretical Framework.* Sacramento: California State Department of Education, Division of Instructional Support and Bilingual Education, Office of Bilingual Bicultural Education, 1981.

Cunningham, Patricia M. *Phonics They Use: Words for Reading and Writing.* New York: Longman, 2000.

Daniels, H. and M. Bizar. *Methods That Matter: Six Structures for Best Practice Classrooms.* York, ME: Stenhouse, 1998.

Day, Frances Ann. *Multicultural Voices in Contemporary Literature: A Resource for Teachers.* Portsmouth, NH: Heinemann, 1994.

DeFord, Diane E., Carol A. Lyons, and Gay Su Pinnell. *Bridges to Literacy: Learning from Reading Recovery.* Portsmouth, NH: Heinemann, 1991.

Dentler, Robert A., and Anne L. Hafner. *Hosting Newcomers: Structuring Educational Opportunities for Immigrant Children.* New York: Teachers College Press, 1997.

Dorn, L., C. French, and T. Jones. *Apprenticeship in Literacy Transitions Across Reading and Writing.* York, ME: Stenhouse, 1998.

Dulay, Heidi, Marina Burt, and Stephen Krashen. *Language Two.* Oxford: Oxford University Press, 1982.

Duthie, C. *True Stories: Nonfiction Literacy in the Primary Classroom.* York, ME: Stenhouse, 1996.

Durgunoglu, A. Y., W. E. Nagy, and B. J. Hancin-Bhatt. "Cross-language of phonological awareness." *Journal of Educational Psychology,* Vol. 85, 453–465, 1993.

Edelsky, C. "Who's Got the Floor?" *Language and Society* 10, 383–421, 1981.

Ellis, R. *Understanding Second Language Acquisition*. Oxford: Oxford University Press, 1985.

Enright, D. S. and M. L. McCloskey. *Integrating English: Developing English Language and Literacy in the Multilingual Classroom*. Reading, MA: Addison-Wesley, 1988.

Escamilla, Kathy. "Teaching Literacy in Spanish." In *The Power of Two Languages 2000: Effective Dual-Language Use Across the Curriculum* edited by J.V. Tinajero and Robert DeVillar. New York: McGraw-Hill, 2000.

Faltis, Christian Jan. *Joinfostering: Adapting Teaching Strategies to the Multilingual Classroom*. New York: Prentice Hall, 1993.

Faltis, Christian, and Sarah Hudelson. "Learning English as an Additional Language in K–12 Schools." *TESOL Quarterly*, vol. 28:3, 1994.

Ferreiro, E. and A. Teberosky. *Literacy Before Schooling*. Portsmouth, NH: Heinemann, 1982.

Fountas, Irene C., and Gay Su Pinnell. *Guided Reading: Good First Teaching for ALL Children*. Portsmouth, NH: Heinemann, 1996.

———. *Matching Books to Readers: Using Leveled Books in Guided Reading, K–3*. Portsmouth, NH: Heinemann, 1999.

Fox, Barbara J. *Strategies for Word Identification*. Columbus: Prentice Hall, Inc, 1996.

Franklin, E. "Encouraging and Understanding the Visual and Written Works of Second-Language Children." In *When They Don't All Speak English: Integrating the ESL Student into the Regular Classroom* edited by P. Rigg and V. Allen. Urbana, IL: National Council of Teachers of English, 1989.

Freeman, David E., and Yvonne S. Freeman. *Teaching Reading in Multilingual Classrooms*. Portsmouth, NH: Heinemann, 2000.

———. *Between Worlds: Access to Second Language Acquisition*. Portsmouth, NH: Heinemann, 1994.

———. *ESL/EFL Teaching: Principles for Success*. Portsmouth, NH: Heinemann, 1998.

Freeman, Yvonne S., and David E. Freeman. *Closing the Achievement Gap: How to Reach Limited Formal Schooling and Long-Term English Learners*. Portsmouth, NH: Heinemann, 2002.

———. *Teaching Reading and Writing in Spanish in the Bilingual Classroom*. Portsmouth, NH: Heinemann, 1997.

Fry, Edward. *Phonics Patterns*. Laguna Beach: Laguna Beach Educational Books, 1996.

Genesee, Fred, ed. *Educating Second Language Children: The Whole Child, the Whole Curriculum, the Whole Community*. Cambridge: Cambridge University Press, 1994.

Gentile, L. "Oral Language: Assessment and Development in Reading Recovery in the United States." In *Research in Reading Recovery* edited by S. Schwartz and A. Klein. Portsmouth, NH: Heinemann, 1997.

Gibbons, Pauline. *Learning to Learn in a Second Language*. Portsmouth, NH: Heinemann, 1993.

Glatthorn, Allan A., et al. *Performance Assessment and Standards-Based Curricula: The Achievement Cycle*. Larchmont, NY: Eye on Education, 1998.

Gottlieb, M. "Promising Assessment Practices for Language Minority Students: National, State, and School Perspectives." *Excellence and Equity for Language Minority Students: Critical Issues and Promising Practices*. Chevy Chase, MD: The Mid-Atlantic Equity Consortium, 2000.

———. *The Language Proficiency Handbook: A Practitioner's Guide to Instructional Assessment*. Springfield: Illinois State Board of Education, 1999.

Griffith, Priscilla L. and Mary W. Olson. "Phonemic Awareness Helps Beginning Readers Break the Code." *The Reading Teacher* 45, No. 7, 1992.

Hadaway, Nancy L., Sylvia M. Vardell, and Terrell A. Young. *Literature-Based Instruction with English Language Learners, K–12*. Boston: Allyn & Bacon, 2002.

Hasbrouck, Jan E. and Carolyn A. Denton. *Phonological Awareness in Spanish: A Summary of Research and Implications for Practice*. In *The Power of Two Languages 2000: Effective Dual-Language Across the Curriculum* edited by J. V. Tinajero and Robert DeVillar. New York: McGraw-Hill, 2000.

Hill, B., L. Norwick, and C. Ruptik. *Classroom Based Assessment*. Norwood, MA: Christopher-Gordon, 1998.

Holdaway, D. *The Foundations of Literacy*. Australia: Ashton Scholastic, 1979.

Holiman, L. *The Complete Guide to Classroom Centers*. Cypress, CA: Creative Teaching Press, 1996.

Holt, D. *Cooperative Learning: A Response to Linguistic and Cultural Diversity*. McHenry, IL: Center for Applied Linguistic/Delta Systems, 1993.

Hudelson, S. *Write On: Children Writing in ESL*. Englewood Cliffs, NJ: Prentice Hall, 1989.

———. "Children's Writing in ESL: What We've Learned, What We're Learning." In *Children and ESL: Integrating Perspectives* edited by P. Rigg and E. S. Enright. Washington, DC: TESOL, 1986.

———. "Kan yo ret an rayt in Ingles: Children Become Literate in English as a Second Language." *TESOL Quarterly* 18, 221–237 (1984).

Johnston, P. *Knowing Literacy: Constructive Literacy Assessment*. York, ME: Stenhouse, 1997.

Kang, Hee-Won. "Helping Second Language Readers Learn from Content Area Text Through Collaboration and Support." *Journal of Reading*, vol. 37:8, 1994.

Keene, Ellin Oliver, and Susan Zimmerman. *Mosaic of Thought: Teaching Comprehension in a Reader's Workshop*. Portsmouth, NH: Heinemann, 1997.

Krashen, S. *Principles and Practice in Second Language Acquisition*. New York: Pergamon Press, 1982.

Krashen, S. and T. Terrell. *The Natural Approach: Language Acquisition in the Classroom*. Hayward, CA: Alemany Press, 1983.

Krashen, S. D. *Fundamentals of Language Education*. Torrence, CA: Laredo, 1992.

Krashen, Stephen. *The Power of Reading: Insights from the Research*. Englewood, CO: Libraries Unlimited, 1993.

———. *Under Attack: The Case Against Bilingual Education*. Culver City, CA: Language Education Associates, 1996.

Kucer, Stephen B., Cecilia Silva, and Esther L. Delgado-Larocco. *Curricular Conversations: Themes in Multilingual and Monolingual Classrooms*. York, ME: Stenhouse, 1995.

Law, Barbara, and Mary Eckes. *Assessment and ESL: A Handbook for K-12 Teachers*. Winnipeg: Peguis, 1995.

Manning, M., G. Manning, and R. Long. *Theme Immersion: Inquiry-Based Curriculum in Elementary and Middle Schools*. Portsmouth, NH: Heinemann, 1994.

McCloskey, Mary Lou. "Literature for Language Learning." <http://www.eslmag.com> *ESL Magazine Online*, November/December 1998.

Miramontes, O. B., A. Nadeau, N. Commins. *Restructuring Schools for Linguistic Diversity: Linking Decision Making to Effective Programs*. New York: Teachers College Press, 1997.

Moline, S. *I See What You Mean: Children at Work with Visual Information*. York, ME: Stenhouse, 1996.

Mooney, Margaret E. *Reading To, With, and By Children*. Katonah, NY: Richard C. Owen Publishers, 1990.

Moustafa, Margaret. *Beyond Traditional Phonics: Research Discoveries and Reading Instructions*. Portsmouth, NH: Heinemann, 1997.

Moustafa, M., and E. Maldonado-Colon: "Whole-to-Parts Phonics Instruction: Building on What Children Know to Help Them Know More." *The Reading Teacher* 52: 448–456, 1999.

National Research Council Institute of Medicine. *Improving Schooling for Language-Minority Children*. Washington, DC: National Academy Press, 1997.

Newkirk, T., ed. *The Teacher as Researcher*. Portsmouth, NH: Heinemann, 1992.

Odlin, Terence. *Language Transfer: Cross-linguistic Influence in Language Learning*. Cambridge: Cambridge University Press, 1989.

Ogbu, J. "Immigrant and Involuntary Minorities in Comparative Perspective." In *Minority Status and Schooling: A Comparative Study of Immigrant and Involuntary Minorities* edited by M. Gibson and J. Ogbu. Garland Publishing: New York, 1991.

Oller, Jr., John W., ed. *Methods That Work: Ideas for Literacy and Language Teachers*. 2d ed. Boston: Heinle & Heinle, 1993.

O'Malley, J., and L. Valdez Pierce. *Authentic Assessment for English Language Learners: Practical Approaches for Teachers*. New York: Addison-Wesley, 1996.

Opitz, Michael F. *Flexible Grouping in Reading: Practical Ways to Help All Students Become Better Readers.* New York: Scholastic Professional Books, 1998.

Opitz, Michael F., ed. *Literary Instruction for Culturally and Linguistically Diverse Students: A Collection of Articles and Commentaries.* Newark: International Reading Association, 1998.

Ovando, C. J., and V. Collier. *Bilingual and ESL Classrooms: Teaching in Multicultural Contexts.* 2d. ed. New York: McGraw-Hill, 1998.

Palincsar, A. S. "The Role of Dialogue in Providing Scaffolded Instruction," *Educational Psychologist* 21 (1 &2), 73–98, 1986.

Parkes, B. *Something Old, Something New: An Integrated Approach to Traditional Tales.* Crystal Lake, IL: Rigby.

———. *Guided Reading with Emergent Readers.* Train the Trainer Seminars, Crystal Lake, IL: Rigby, 1997.

Payne, C. and M. Schulman. *Getting the Most Out of Morning Message and Other Shared Writing Lessons.* New York: Scholastic, 1998.

Pearson, P.D. "Focus on Research: Teaching and Learning Reading, A Research Perspective." *Language Arts* (October), 505, 1993.

Peregoy, Suzanne F., and Owen F. Boyle. *Reading, Writing, and Learning in ESL: A Resource Book for K–12 Teachers.* 2d ed. White Plains, NY: Longman, 1997.

Peyton, Joy Kreeft, and Leslee Reed. *Dialogue Journal Writing with Nonnative English Speakers: A Handbook for Teachers.* Alexandria, VA: TESOL Publications, 1990.

Pinnell, Gay Su, et al. *Word Matters: Teaching Phonics and Spelling in the Reading/Writing Classroom.* Portsmouth, NH: Heinemann, 1998.

Power, B. *Taking Note: Improving Your Observational Notetaking.* York, ME: Stenhouse, 1997.

Power, B. and R. Hubbard, eds. *Oops: What We Learn When Our Teaching Fails.* York, ME: Stenhouse, 1996.

Reeves, D. B. *Making Standards Work,* 2d ed. Denver, CO: Advanced Learning Centers, 1998.

Rigg, Pat, and D. Scott Enright, eds. *Children and ESL: Integrating Perspectives.* Alexandria, VA: TESOL Publications, 1986.

Rogoff, B. *Apprenticeship in Thinking: Cognitive Development in Social Contexts.* New York: Oxford University Press, 1990.

Royce, Terry. "Multimodality in the TESOL Classroom: Exploring Visual-Verbal Synergy." *TESOL Quarterly* 36, no. 2, 191–205, 2002.

Samway, Katharine Davies, and Denise McKeon, eds. *Common Threads of Practice: Teaching English to Children Around the World.* Alexandria, VA: TESOL Publications, 1993.

Samway, Katharine Davies, and Denise McKeon. *Myths and Realities: Best Practices for Language Minority Students.* Portsmouth, NH: Heinemann, 1999.

Schiffini, A. "Language, Literacy, and Content Instruction: Strategies for Teachers." In *Kids Come in All Languages: Reading Instruction for ESL Students* edited by K. Spandenburg-Urbschat, and R. Pritchard. Newark: International Reading Association, 1994.

Schinke-Llano, Linda, and Rebecca Rauff, eds. *New Ways in Teaching Young Children.* Alexandria, VA: TESOL Publications, 1996.

Short, D.J., et al. *Training Others to Use the ESL Standards: A Professional Development Manual.* Alexandria, VA: TESOL, 2000.

Short, K. G., J. C. Harste, and C. Burke. *Creating Classrooms for Authors and Inquirers.* 2d ed. Portsmouth, NH: Heinemann, 1996.

Smallwood, Betty Ansin, ed. *Integrating the ESL Standards Into Classroom Practice: Grades Pre-K–2.* Alexandria, VA: TESOL, 2000.

Spangenberg-Urbschat, Karen, and Robert Pritchard. *Kids Come in All Languages: Reading Instruction for ESL Students.* Newark: International Reading Association, 1994.

Sparks, D. and Hirsch, S. *A New Vision for Staff Development.* Alexandria, VA: Association for Supervision and Curriculum Development, 1997.

Stahl, S. and B. Murray. "Defining Phonological Awareness and Its Relationship to Early Reading." *Journal of Educational Psychology* 86, Vol. 2, 221–234, 1994.

Stahl, Steven. "Saying the 'P' Word: Nine Guidelines for Exemplary Phonics Instruction." *The Reading Teacher* 45, no. 8, 618–625, 1992.

Stanovich, Keith E. "Romance and Reality." *The Reading Teacher* 47, no. 4, 280–291, 1992.

Stefanakis, E. *Whose Judgment Counts? Assessing Bilingual Children K–3.* Portsmouth, NH: Heinemann, 1998.

Swan, Michael, and Bernard Smith. *Learner English: A Teacher's Guide to Interference and Other Problems.* Cambridge: Cambridge University Press, 1987.

Teachers of English to Speakers of Other Languages. *ESL Standards for Pre-K–12 Scenarios for ESL Standards-Based Assessment.* Alexandria, VA: TESOL Publications, 2001.

———. *ESL Standards for Pre-K–12 Students.* Alexandria, VA: TESOL Publications, 1997.

Tharp, R. and R. Gallimore. *Rousing Minds to Life: Teaching, Learning, and Schooling in Social Context.* Cambridge: Cambridge University Press.

Thomas, Wayne, and Virginia Collier. *School Effectiveness for Language Minority Students.* Washington, DC: National Clearinghouse for Bilingual Education, 1997.

Tierney, Robert J., John E. Readence, and Ernest K. Dishner. *Reading Strategies and Practices: A Compendium.* 4th ed. Boston: Allyn & Bacon, 1995.

Tinajero, J., S. R. Hurley, and E. V. Lozano. *Developing Language and Literacy in Bilingual Classrooms.* In *Educating Latino Students: A Guide to Successful Practice* edited by M. L. Gonzales et al. Lancaster, PA: Technomics. 143–160, 1998.

Tomlinson, Carol Ann. "Grading for Success." *Educational Leadership* 58, no. 6, 2000.

Traill, Leana. *Highlight My Strengths.* Crystal Lake, IL: Rigby, 1995.

Trelease, Jim. *The Read-Aloud Handbook.* New York: Penguin Books, 1985.

Valdés, Guadalupe. *Con Respeto: Bridging the Distances Between Culturally Diverse Families and Schools.* New York: Teachers College Press, 1996.

Vale, David, with Anne Feunteun. *Teaching Children English: A Training Course for Teachers of English to Children.* Cambridge: Cambridge University Press, 1995.

Vygotsky, L. S. *Thought and Language.* Cambridge, MA: MIT Press, 1962.

———. *Mind in Society.* Cambridge, MA: Harvard University Press, 1978.

Wagstaff, Janiel. *Phonics That Work: New Strategies for the Reading/Writing Classroom.* New York: Scholastic, 1996.

Waterland, L. *Read With Me: An Apprenticeship Approach to Reading.* Stroud, UK: Thimble Press, 1985.

White, Lydia. *Universal Grammar and Second Language Acquisition.* Philadelphia: John Benjamin Publishing, 1989.

Wiggins, G. *Educative Assessment.* San Francisco, CA: Jossey-Bass, 1998.

Wilde, Sandra. *What's a Schwa Sound Anyway?* Portsmouth, NH: Heinemann, 1997.

Wink, Joan. *Critical Pedagogy: Notes from the Real World.* 2d ed. White Plains, NY: Longman, 1999.

Wong-Fillmore, L., and C. Valadez. *Teaching bilingual learners.* In *Handbook of Research on Teaching* edited by M. Wittrock. Washington, DC: American Educational Research Association, 648–685, 1985.

Yopp, Hallie K. "A Test for Assessing Phonemic Awareness in Young Children." *The Reading Teacher* 49, no. 1, 20–29, 1995.

———. "Developing phonemic awareness in young children." *The Reading Teacher* 45, no. 9, pp. 696–707, 1992.

Teacher Notes

Teacher Notes

Teacher Notes